FASCINATING FUNGI
OF THE NORTH WOODS

Second Edition

Written by
CORA MOLLEN & LARRY WEBER

Illustrated by
RICK KOLLATH & BONNIE WENBORG

Kollath+Stensaas Publishing
394 Lake Avenue South, Suite 406
Duluth, MN 55802
Office: 218.727.1731
Orders: 800.678.7006
info@kollathstensaas.com
www.kollathstensaas.com

FASCINATING FUNGI *of the* NORTH WOODS:
2nd EDITION

Printed in Canada by Friesens
10 9 8 7 6 5 4 3 2   Second Edition, Second Printing 2023

Graphic Designer: Rick Kollath
Editorial Director: Mark Sparky Stensaas

ISBN-13: 978-1-936571-03-1

ACKNOWLEDGEMENTS

I am grateful to my daughter, Anne Small, for her knowledge and advice which helped shape the texts, and for her computer know-how, which was indispensable. I want to thank all the members of the Northstate Mycological Club, for putting into my hands, over the years, thousands of North Woods mushrooms for discussion and study. Each member contributed to the broadening of my understanding of fungi and their role in the natural environment. Special thanks to the photographers among them, whose images captured the elements of mushroom's form and color that influenced my descriptions of various species. Thanks to educators, Pat Folgert, Carol Lanphear-Cook, Dana Richter, Daniel Czederpiltz and Stephen Nelsen. I am particularly grateful to Mark Sparky Stensaas, Larry Weber and Rick Kollath, who gave me the opportunity to contribute to this book. It was from the start their idea, and is the fruit of lots of planning and personal effort on their part.

Sincere thanks to the experts and authors whose writings have provided grounding and substance for the descriptions in this mushroom guide: George Baron, Gary N. Lincoff, George W. Hudler, Alexander H. Smith, Alan and Aleen Bessette, Kent and Vera McKnight, Tom Volk, David Fisher, Oscar K. Miller, David Arora, Roger Phillips, Verne Graham, Michael Kao, Bryce Kendrick and Steve Nelsen.

Cora Mollen
February 2, 2012

The best way to learn about the local mushrooms and other fungi is to take frequent walks in the woods during late summer and autumn. Having an expert with you helps, and I thank some wonderful teachers of workshops that have helped me identify fungal finds. Cora Mollen (my co-author), Anne Small, Mike MacCall and Tom Volk have all given their expertise to mushroom classes I've attended. The Minnesota Mycological Society was able to help identify several of my photos. The best way to learn is to teach, and the seventh grade natural science students at the Marshall School in Duluth, Minnesota have helped me learn through their many questions. I always appreciate their enthusiasm. Also several garden clubs, Hartley Nature Center and many other organizations have allowed me to speak about mushrooms.

As usual, Mark Sparky Stensaas did his terrific and patient editing, while Rick Kollath and Bonnie Wenborg provided the excellent and detailed illustrations. My wife, Frannie was supportive in letting me pursue this activity. Have a great fungi walk!

Larry A. Weber
February 6, 2012

CONTENTS & CHECKLIST

To my husband Roy,
who encouraged the writing and was admirably patient with my piles of
books, scatterings of notepaper and hours of focus on the fungi.

And

To a son and daughter whose enthusiasm for their natural surroundings
caught hold of me, and eventually brought me to the study of mushrooms.

And

To Edward and Alice Polasek, whose love for mushrooming and wise advice
were a support and joy across the years.

—Cora

To Frannie,
my companion in life and on many mushroom walks.

And

To the students, faculty and staff at the Marshall School in Duluth, Minnesota
where I was privileged to teach for 30 years.

—Larry

MUSHROOMS, an INTRODUCTION

What is a Mushroom?

The structure that we call a mushroom, the umbrella-shaped growth in woods, yards and parks, is only the reproductive part (sometimes called the **fruiting body**) of a much larger fungal organism. While these fleshy parts sometimes grow huge or in big clusters, they are only a portion of the fungus—the part that holds the spores. In this sense, they could be compared to an apple on a tree and, like picking the apple from the tree doesn't harm the tree, so picking a mushroom does not hurt the whole fungus.

Fungi (plural of fungus) are a very large and diverse group of organisms. They are neither plant nor animal. Like the plants, they appear to have parts such as roots, stems and branches and they are non-mobile. But unlike green plants, they cannot make their own food and so need to act like animals to get required nutrition from other sources. Modern classification treats fungi as its own kingdom though very old texts will call fungi plants.

Not all fungi are mushrooms. The word "mushroom" is often used in describing any of various fungi with fleshy fruiting bodies. This means that fungi such as molds, mildews and yeasts are clearly not mushrooms, but in a wide interpretation, any fleshy fungi; including puffballs, brackets, corals, morels and cups may be called mushrooms.

Since gilled fungi tend to be a large and common group, this book will divide all those listed as either gilled or non-gilled. Gilled fungi are the mushrooms that hold these blade-like growths, called gills, under the cap. Non-gilled fungi are all the rest: boletes (pore mushrooms), tooth mushrooms, brackets, corals, puffballs, jellies and sac fungi.

Mushroom Parts

Most of us think of a mushroom as an umbrella-shaped structure sticking up from the ground. But the part that we see is only the fruiting body (reproductive stage) of the mushroom. Most of the fungus is under ground in long thin

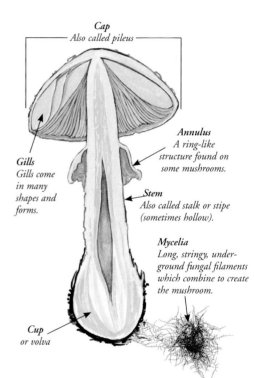

Cap
Also called pileus

Annulus
A ring-like structure found on some mushrooms.

Gills
Gills come in many shapes and forms.

Stem
Also called stalk or stipe (sometimes hollow).

Mycelia
Long, stringy, underground fungal filaments which combine to create the mushroom.

Cup
or volva

growths called **mycelia**. This, as well as the entire mushroom anatomy, is composed of minute hair-like structures known as **hyphae**.

The most obvious part of the mushrooms is the cap. **Caps** are often flat and round, but they can be conical, bell-shaped or vase-shaped too. They vary in color and may be brown, gray, white, yellow, red, purple or any other color in the rainbow. Many have patches or warts on the surface that show what's left of the **veil** that once surrounded the immature mushroom (the "button") when it first grew above ground.

Under the cap are the **gills**; blade-like parts upon which the **spores** grow. Seen only with a microscope, the spores develop on tiny club-like structures called **basidia**. It is from these that the mature spores will drop and disperse. Gills sometimes attach to the stem at forty-five degree angles (**adnexed**), at right angles (**adnate**) or extend down the stalk (**decurrent**).

GILL ATTACHMENT

Gills

Free: Gills not attached to stalk.

Decurrent: Gills run down the stem.

Adnate: Gills attach to the stalk at right angles.

Adnexed: Gills attach to the stalk at forty-five degree angles.

Notched: Gills indent before joining stalk.

Others have gills not even touching the stalk (**free**). Gills may be tightly packed together or widely spaced. In place of gills some mushrooms have **teeth**, **spines** or they have tubes with holes called **pores**. All of these serve a similar function, as do the gills.

Typically, the cap sits on top of a centrally located **stem** (**stalk or stipe**). But, especially for those that grow on wood, the stalk may be off-center or even non-existent. Stalks vary in size and thickness. Many species of mushrooms have a ring (**annulus**); a band-like growth around the stalk.

The **ring** is what is left by a **partial veil** (a growth connecting the cap to the stalk which covers the developing gills). It gets torn by the developing

COMMON MUSHROOM CAP SHAPES

Flat   *Round*   *Bell-shaped*   *With Central Knob*   *Depressed*   *Conical*   *Vase-shaped*

TYPES OF GILLS

Equal: *Gills all the same size*

Crowded: *Gills set close together.*

Distant: *Gills widely spaced*

Varying Lengths: *Gills of uneven lengths*

mushroom and remnants stay on the stalk as a ring. Some species have a cup (volva) at the base of the stalk. This cup stays with the mature mushroom as a sign of the earlier universal veil that covered the entire emerging button stage. For many mushrooms, we only see the cap, gills and stalk. A few others also have rings and cups.

Mushroom Life Cycle

Mushrooms reproduce by forming small, usually single-celled structures called **spores**. These spores may drop from the undersides of a cap or other type of spore-bearing structure. The spores serve these purposes:

1. They are reproductive and capable of growing a new organism.

2. They are agents of dispersal.

3. They are able to go dormant for long periods until favorable conditions allow for growth.

When finding such favorable conditions—usually moisture and enough nutrients—spores germinate by growing a single filament (**hypha**). This soon proliferates to a mass of tissue (**mycelium**) that is able to penetrate into substrates; usually dead plant material. This vegetative growth may last for months or years until proper conditions are present to begin forming fruiting bodies. The reproductive phase starts when a hypha from one mycelium merges with another. This may be female and male or merely two different strains. The mushroom grows from this union.

Basidiomycetes

Knotted forms of hyphae begin to push above the ground. The young mushrooms, sometimes called buttons, may look like chicken eggs when they first emerge. Some buttons have a cover over all parts. This **universal veil** breaks as it grows. Parts may stick to the cap, later appearing as **warts**, while lower portions are responsible for the volva at the base of the stalk.

MATURITY OF A TYPICAL MUSHROOM

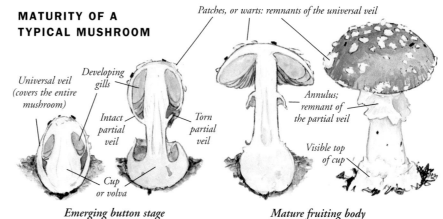

Patches, or warts: remnants of the universal veil

Universal veil (covers the entire mushroom)

Developing gills

Intact partial veil

Torn partial veil

Annulus; remnant of the partial veil

Visible top of cup

Cup or volva

Emerging button stage

Mature fruiting body

BASIDIOMYCETES

Spores develop on club-shaped basidia.

Spores (highly magnified)

Basidia

Basidia along gills

Basidia in tubes

Basidia on "teeth"

Basidia in ridges of outer surface

Basidia in loose inner tissue

ASCOMYCETES

Spores develop in tube-shaped asci.

Spores (highly magnified)

Asci

Asci in pits

Asci on inner surface

Fleshy fungi break down into two groups based on how their spores are produced.

As the mushroom matures, a new growth of spores develops on minute, club-shaped organs called **basidia** which cover the sides of the gills. Usually, four spores grow on each basidium. A mushroom's many gills provides surface area for millions of spores to form and to be dispersed.

Most fleshy fungi produce spores on basidia (**Basidiomycota**). These include the gill mushrooms, tooth mushrooms, pore mushrooms, brackets, puffballs, corals and jelly fungi.

Ascomycetes

Others produce spores in sacs called **asci** (singular: **ascus**).

In place of gills some mushrooms have teeth or spines (left) or they have tubes with holes called pores (right).

These **Ascomycota** are often called **sac fungi**. Members of this group include the morels, cup fungi, dead man's fingers, jelly babies and lobster fungi. With maturity, these sacs open and spores are shot into the air. A cloud of spores can be produced by bumping these fungi as often happens with wind or rain.

Slimy Sex

The life cycle of the **slime molds** (**Myxomycota**) is different from the Basidiomycota or Ascomycota. It is now believed that they are not fungi at all. Most of the time, they live hidden in well-rotted wood or leaves. When moisture and temperature allows for fruiting, they put out a slimy mass of protoplasm (**plasmodium**) that may travel to an appropriate site to reproduce. The amoeboid movement is slow, but quite noticeable, often after a summer rain. As they move, they will engulf organic particles as nutrients. Once established, the plasmodial stage becomes the sporangia that forms tiny fruiting bodies covered with spores.

SYMBIOTIC MUSHROOM/TREE RELATIONSHIP

Mycorrhizae (fungal "roots") take carbohydrates from the tree's roots in exchange for soil nutrients the tree can't get by itself.

The mushroom is only the fruiting body of the mycorrhizae; these small fibers make up the main organism.

Tree roots

Ecology and Habitat

Once a fungus begins growing a mycelium, it needs to get nutrients. For mushrooms, it is usually one, or a combination, of three methods. Most fungi are **saprophytic**—feed on dead material, usually plants. A large number are **mycorrhizal** or mutualistic in their relationship with plants, including trees. A few are **parasitic**, whereby they gain nutrients from another living organism.

Eaters of the Dead

Saprophytic mushrooms, also called **saprobes**, use enzymes to break down dead matter and use the available biotic material to carry on their existence.

The dead and decaying matter is usually some form of wood: logs, branches, twigs, wood chips, sawdust, or it may even be dead parts of a living tree such as the outer bark and inner wood. Others gather nutrition from rotting leaves, needles, manure, pine cones or even other mushrooms. Moisture or wet conditions are needed to carry on such action.

Partners to the End

Mycorrhizal, or **mutualistic** relationships frequently exist with trees, often these are specific. Small hyphae, called mycorrhizae are the basis of this partnership. These form a mantle or sheath around the minute tree rootlets. Here a net of hyphae develop and they exchange needed nutrition. Fungi obtain sugars from the tree, while the tree gets nutrients and increased water uptake in return. With such a deeply established relationship, the mushrooms can only grow around the appropriate trees. This symbiosis is easy to note when observing the same species of mushrooms at the same place for many years.

Selfish Friends

Parasitic fungi are highly variable and may exist on a huge number of hosts, including animals, even humans. Some **parasitic mushrooms** attack trees.

Saprophytic mushrooms obtain nutrients by using enzymes to break down dead and decaying plant matter.

Parasites live off a host plant, endangering the host's health as it grows. The tree may eventually die but in the process create new habitats for many other organisms.

Being a successful parasite means not killing the host quickly. Many of these parasites live on a host for years and eventually weaken it to the point of killing it.

Some take nutrition and water from the plant while others make toxins. The surface mushroom is only the fruiting body of a mycelial growth that may go on throughout much of the body of the host.

Where Fungi Live

Because of their relationship to trees, either saprophytic, mycorrhizal or parasitic, mushrooms are most common around them. They thrive in deciduous, coniferous or mixed forests but can also be found in parks, yards, on wood chip trails or on stumps where trees used to grow.

Mushrooms can also be found in open fields or lawns. Those feeding on animal dung thrive while a few others take advantage of dead plant material. Bogs and swamps, where a continuous amount of moisture is regularly available, harbor their own specific mushroom types as well.

Collecting Mushrooms

Ideally, we would all be able to identify all the mushrooms we find in the field. Because of the huge variety of mushrooms, this is hard to do and so we often need to collect some and bring them home for a closer look. Remember that when you collect a mushroom, you are collecting only the fruiting body and not hurting the entire underground growth of mycelia. Even so, it is best to take only a few mature specimens.

Most collectors find that picnic baskets make excellent mushroom carriers. Plastic buckets or paper bags have been used too. Each specimen should be put into a small paper bag, waxed sandwich bag or waxed paper. Don't use plastic bags—they tend to hasten decay.

An iPhone, digital voice recorder, small notebook or three-by-five cards are useful to record data such as habitat, type of trees nearby, whether it is growing singularly, scattered or in clusters and any other pertinent information. Many collectors place written notes directly in the bag with the mushrooms.

Most mushrooms can be cut off, dug out or removed from woody substrates with a knife. It is wise to put a colorful flag or cloth on the knife to keep it from being lost.

The majority of mushrooms in our region have their fruiting time in late summer or early autumn. Collecting in August or September is nearly always a successful venture. Their growth and development is highly influenced by the weather: going out two to five days after a significant rain may be the best time. But even during dry years, with some searching fungi can be found.

Mushroom Identification

Look for a combination of traits when identifying mushrooms, including

Spore print of an Amanita.

cap shape, size and color; how gills are attached to the stalk; stalk texture, length, diameter, shape and color; whether there's a ring around the stalk or a cup at the base; what color the flesh bruises when cut; if the gills exude latex when cut. In addition, we should record the date, habitat, type of substrate, and if the mushrooms grow singly, scattered or in clustered groups. Now consult this book in addition to others listed under *Titles of Interest*.

Making Spore Prints

Though all these criteria work well for determining the mushroom's family or genus, we often must take identification one step further and make a spore print. In gilled mushrooms, spores grow on the gills under the cap. It is from here that the spores fall. Spores are species-specific and can be highly effective in identification.

Making a spore print is easy and though procedures vary, this method works well. Select good mature specimen to use. Take off the cap by cutting through the stalk at the site where they meet. Put the cap on paper with gills down. A half-black-half-white piece of paper works best if you don't know whether the spores are dark or light. The cap is then covered with a glass or cup. This limits air movement so spores fall directly onto the paper. The mushroom cap is then left in this position for two to six hours—preferably overnight.

The resulting spore print on the paper is valuable for determining the mushroom's genus or even species. Many books are put together based on the color of the spore print. In this book we place an icon of the color of the spore print next to all the gilled fungi and boletes. Anyone serious about further identification of mushrooms will need to collect some, bring them home and make spore prints. Though they work best for gilled fungi and boletes, they can also be made with chanterelles, tooth fungi, corals and brackets (shelf fungi).

HOW TO MAKE A SPORE PRINT

1. Remove the stalk and place the mushroom gill-side down on a piece of paper.

Note: you can tape together white and black paper if you don't know if the spores will be light or dark.

2. Cover the cap with a glass cup or bowl.

3. Leave the cap in position 2-6 hours or even overnight (ideal).

3. Voile! A spore print.

A Key to Some Common Groups of Fungi

Typical Mushrooms (with cap & stem)

With gills

Spores white — gills free

gills attached

With teeth — **Hydnums**
With teeth, not gills
Page 88

Spores yellow-brown — **Paxillus**
Gills decurrent
Pages 26, 62

With ridges — **Chanterelles**
With ridges, not gills
Page 81

Spores purple-brown to chocolate

spores purple-brown — **Stropharia**
On wood, dung
Pages 31, 70

spores chocolate — **Agaricus**
On grass
Pages 44-45

Spores black — **Coprinus**
Dissolves to black goo. Gills free.
Pages 42-43

With pores — **Boletes**
Fleshy, usually on ground
Pages 72-78

Polypores
Leathery, on wood
Pages 87, 110-118

Spores rusty to cinnamon

on wood — **Pholiota**
Scales on cap
Page 52

on ground — **Cortinarius**
Veil like spider web when young
Pages 35-38

Spores pink to salmon — gills free

Based on a key in North American Mushrooms *by Orson Miller Jr. 2006.*

Amanita
Volva present
Pages 12-17

Lepiota
No volva
Pages 45, 71

Hygrophorus
Waxy. Often bright colors
Pages 39-41

Russula
Brittle flesh
Pages 18-21

Lactarius
Exudes latex when cut
Pages 32-34

Armillaria
Clusters at base of trees
Pages 60-61

volva present **Volvariella**
On wood
Page 57

volva absent **Pluteus**
On wood
Page 58

Other Fungi

Corals
Pages 89-93, 121

Clubs, etc.
Pages 90-92

Jellies
Pages 104-105, 109

Black Knot
Page 118

Bird's-Nests
Pages 100-101

Hericiums
Pages 120-121

Puffballs
Pages 96-99

Morels
Pages 82-83

Earthstars
Page 99

False Morels
Pages 84-86

Stinkhorns
Pages 94-95

Cups
Pages 100, 102, 105-107

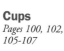

THE QUESTION OF EDIBILITY

Wild mushrooms can be the most delectable addition to a meal, but some mushrooms are poisonous, and they may resemble edible species. Eating them may make you sick or, in very rare instances, kill you.

It is your responsibility to identify any wild fungi with 100 percent certainty before you eat it. If at all possible, your first few fungi forages should be with a knowledgeable and experienced mycologist.

Enthusiasm for mushroom hunting is often spurred by the hope of finding some wild delicacies for the table. Such enthusiasm must be moderated by care, experience and education. There's no need for a phobic fear of wild mushrooms, but it's important to be aware that certain mushrooms contain toxic compounds. Some of these toxins may be life-threatening; others are less dangerous, but capable of giving an unwary eater some very unpleasant moments. Only those mushrooms that are positively identified as good edibles should be eaten. A person may be guided by cultural familiarity with certain mushrooms.

Formal classroom and field study with a knowledgeable teacher and use of detailed guide books can provide a basis for making accurate identifications. Some mushrooms are distinctive and well-known edibles and make a good starting point for beginners who intend to try wild mushrooms as food. Mushrooms, like other foods, can evoke individual allergic reactions, so an apt motto is "proceed with caution." Start with tiny portions to see how YOUR body reacts. The choice to eat wild mushrooms is an individual one. The individual who makes that choice is responsible for the consequences. This book is not intended to be a guide to edibility. Eat at your own risk!

Check the *Titles of Interest* for other books on identification and edibility of mushrooms.

 This icon is reserved for the best-of-the-best edible mushrooms. But you still need to use caution when identifying.

 Don't even think of eating mushrooms with this icon. Though probably not deadly, eating them can cause serious illness.

 The skull-and-crossbones icon means this fungus can be deadly if ingested! Stay away!

How To Use This Guide

We've written this book to pique the interest of all nature lovers who come upon fungi in their forays afield. Often overlooked and much maligned, our North Woods fungi are a fascinating group. In these pages you'll meet a puffball that can be as big as a basketball, an *Amanita* that Viking warriors ingested before battle and the world's largest living organism.

We could not include all the species of fungi found in the North Woods—there are literally thousands of species—but we tried to include the mushrooms you're likely to notice in the field. We not only included very common species but also not-so-common species that are either uniquely shaped, huge, colorful or just plain bizarre. IBMs (little brown mushrooms) were ignored completely; even experts cannot agree on their classification. We also skipped such annoying fungi as Athlete's Foot and cheese mold. Sorry.

Fascinating Fungi of the North Woods is not arranged by color or phylogenetic order but rather is divided into six easy-to-remember categories [Listed on the upper left hand page of each spread.]:

- ❖ **Gilled on Ground** (including lawns)
- ❖ **Gilled on Wood** (rotten logs, living trees, wood chips, stumps)
- ❖ **Gilled on Other** (pine cones, leaves, animal dung, other fungi)
- ❖ **Non-gilled on Ground**
- ❖ **Non-gilled on Wood**
- ❖ **Non-gilled on Other**

Within these categories, fungi are arranged by genus and similar forms. When you find a fungus, first try and put it into one of the above categories. Note any characteristics, maybe make a spore print, and grab your copy of *Fascinating Fungi* to find your fungus. Happy hunting!

Check left page header for the category of mushroom (e.g. Gilled on Ground.)

We use the most well known regional common name and the most recent scientific name to identify each species.

Phenograms let you know when that fungus may be found in the field.

Captions point out identification traits to look for in the field.

Size icons show the range of cap widths and stalk heights.

***EDIBILITY ICONS** See previous page for notes on icons denoting poisonous and choice edible mushrooms*

Stylized icons show gill spacing (from below) and gill attachment (side view). [See introduction for explanation of terms.]

Inset illustrations and sidebars highlight unique natural history.

This icon shows the color of a typical spore print. Shape, of course, will vary.

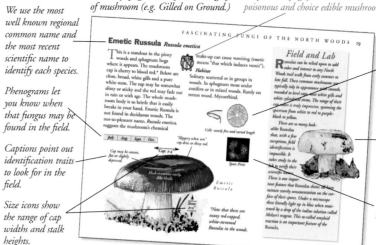

FASCINATING FUNGI OF THE NORTH WOODS 19

Emetic Russula *Russula emetica*

This is a standout in the piney woods and sphagnum bogs where it appears. The mushroom cap is cherry to blood red.* Below are close, broad, white gills and a pure white stem. The cap may be somewhat slimy or sticky and the red may fade out in rain or with age. The whole mushroom body is so brittle that it easily breaks in your hand. Emetic Russula is not found in deciduous woods. The not-so-pleasant name, *Russula emetica*, suggests the mushroom's chemical make-up can cause vomiting (*emetic* means "that which induces vomit").

Habitat
Solitary, scattered or in groups in woods. In sphagnum moss under conifers or in mixed woods. Rarely on rotten wood. Mycorrhizal.

Field and Lab

Russulas can be relied upon to add color and interest to any North Woods trail walk from early summer to late fall. These common mushrooms are typically tidy in appearance with smooth, rounded to level caps, often white gills and white colored stems. The range of their colors is truly impressive, spanning the spectrum from white to red to purple-black to yellow.

There are as many look-alike Russulas that, with a few exceptions, field identification is impossible. It takes study in the lab to verify their scientific identity.

There is one important feature that Russulas share — a minute starchy ornamentation on the surface of their spores. Under a microscope these literally light up in blue when moistened by a drop of the iodine solution called Melzer's reagent. This so-called amyloid reaction is an important feature of the Russulas.

Gills: nearly free and varied length.

"Slippery when wet" cap dries to shiny red.

Cap may be convex, flat or slightly depressed.

Flesh crumbles easily, like chalk.

Emetic Russula

Spore Print

Note that there are many red-capped, white-stemmed Russulas in the woods.

GILLED *on* GROUND

Gilled fungi are the stereo-typical mushrooms that we all started drawing in second grade; they have a stalk and a cap with gills underneath.

More specifically, they have spores that are attached to miniscule club-shaped organs called basidia on the gills. There are thousands of species and colored like the rainbow: orange, purple, red, white, blue, green. We've only included the well-known, the most fascinating and the gaudiest species.

Be sure to check the base of the mushroom to make sure that it is growing from the soil and not attached to rotten wood. If so, check the next section "Gilled on Wood."

Fly Amanita *Amanita muscaria* var. *formosa*

We tend to think of Fly Amanita as a mushroom with a bright red cap speckled with white. While this is certainly true in the Rocky Mountains, Alaska and Pacific Northwest, in the North Woods it is normally yellowish-orange with white specks. The white flecks on the cap are actually remnants of the white veil that covered the developing mushroom. A bulbous stem base hides just below the surface soil. Gills are whitish, crowded and not attached to the stem. Some are full length and others half-length. Ring is high on the stalk and the volva is mostly gone at the base.

White "scabs" are actually remnant patches of the veil that once covered the developing mushroom.

Cap: 3-10"

A yellow-orange cap is the signature of the variation formosa found in the upper Midwest and Great Lakes region.

Caps may be as large as a dinner plate.

Stem: 3–7"

Look for the diagnostic ring on the stem.

Fly Amanita

| June | July | Aug. | Sept. | Oct. |

Habitat

Scattered to grouped, usually gregarious, in woods under aspen, poplar, birch, pine, spruce and fir. Mycorrhizal with birch, aspen and spruce. They may be found in mixed forests but are usually on acidic soils.

A circumpolar species that spans North America, Scandinavia and Russia. Found in North America from Alaska to Labrador and south to North Carolina and the Rocky Mountains.

Fungal Fly Swatter

The name Fly Amanita comes from the belief that a saucer of milk mixed with a cap of *Amanita muscaria* can stun or kill flies. Even in Norway it is called *Rød Fluesopp* or "red fly mushroom."

Viking Vice

Rumor has it that the Vikings of the eleventh and twelfth centuries revered

Gills:
crowded and free

Spore Print

Amanita muscaria. One of its side effects is said to be brief periods of superhuman strength sometimes followed by coma-like sleep and possibly death. Could this have been the Vikings' secret in battle?

Alice in Wonderland

Toxins atropine and muscarine combine in Fly Amanita to cause symptoms of intoxication and on rare occasions, death. Symptoms would be much more severe if the two toxins did not tend to neutralize each other. Lewis Caroll, author of *Alice in Wonderland*, was a known experimenter with drugs. The white-spotted red mushroom illustrated in his book is most likely Fly Amanita. Is it possible that Caroll took Amanita and experienced its hallucinogenic effects? Would this explain small things appearing large in the story…and other bizarre details?

Lovely but Lethal

A full 90 percent of all fatal mushroom poisonings have been attributed to amanitas and their deadly amatoxins. Amatoxins cause severe, life threatening illness. If even a small portion of a mushroom that contains amatoxins is eaten, the powerful toxins act on the cell system of the body blocking vital production of new cells. Liver and kidney failure and death can result. The symptoms of the poisoning are delayed; occurring six to eight hours after the poisonous mushroom was eaten. Then nausea, vomiting, fever and tremors take hold. These may be bad enough to cause hospitalization. But the symptoms are temporary and may be passed off as a case of simple food poisoning. (That's why recent consumption of mushrooms should always be mentioned to the attending doctor) Three to six days later, however, there are symptoms of liver failure. By that time, the toxins have done much internal damage to liver, kidneys, intestines as well as heart and brain.

Destroying Angel *Amanita virosa*

This tall, robust, pure white mushroom has a pristine appearance. The large cap is convex then nearly flat with a raised center and clean, unlined margin. Its surface is smooth without ornamentation and has a satiny, shimmering quality. The white gills are close and free. They are narrow to somewhat broad and sometimes with a powdery look. Shorter gills mix with full-length gills.

The partial veil is membranous and breaks to form a thin skirt-like ring on the upper stem. The ring is delicate, gets tattered and sometimes disappears.

The stem is thick, tapering upward and with a small ball-like base. A large white volva encases the stem base. The volva's upper edges are free from the stem and often scalloped. It may be necessary to dig into the soil to uncover the volva. The mushroom has a yeast-like odor.

Habitat

Usually found in mixed woods, but fruiting also occurs in open areas with sandy acidic soil and an edging of trees.

Pernicious Poisoner

This mushroom is said to be the most deadly mushroom in eastern North America. Besides *Amanita virosa*, there are two white, dangerous look-alikes, *A. bisporigera* and *A. verna*. The three can only be distinguished from one another by chemical and microscopic exam. Unfortunately, to date, there is no specific antidote to amatoxins. Treatment involves attempts to stabilize and sustain the victim and to clear the toxins from the body (see sidebar on previous page).

Physician, Heal Thyself

French physician and researcher, Dr. P. Bastien developed a method of treatment that he used to save a number of amatoxin victims. Later, to test and verify the efficacy of the treatment, Bastien twice consumed amatoxin-containing mushrooms and then set to cure himself. That's dedication to research! The

Cap: 2-5"

Look for tattered, thin skirt-like ring on the upper stem.

Stem: 3–8"

Angel of Death

You may have to dig for it, but look for the large white volva that encases the stem base. It is often free at the upper edges and may be scalloped.

| June | July | Aug. | Sept. | Oct. |

Bastien method is the chief amatoxin treatment used in France.

It is a three-part treatment: 1. Intravenous injections of one gram of vitamin C twice daily; 2. Two capsules of nifuroxazide three times daily; 3. Two tablets of dihydrostreptomycin three times a day. Penicillin, fluid control and electrolyte balance supplement the treatment.

The Meixner Test

The easy way to test a mushroom for amatoxins is called the Meixner Test. Draw a circle on newsprint paper. Press the liquid out of a piece of fresh mushroom into the circle and allow it to dry. When dry, put a drop of concentrated hydrochloric acid on the circle. If amatoxins are present, a blue color will develop within 20 minutes. The more amatoxins present, the quicker the blue reaction.

Gills: crowded and free

Spore Print

Tawny Grisette *Amanita fulva*

A classic beauty with simple "tailored" lines. It has a broadly bell-shaped cap, long tapering stem and pale sheath-like volva. The cap is orange, orange-brown to red brown with a smooth rather glossy surface and deeply lined margin. Mature caps are flat with a raised center. The white to cream-colored gills are broad, closely packed under the cap and free from the stem. The mushroom's

Spore Print

firm stem is tapered upward. It has a white, even surface with faint hints of cap color and a covering of very fine white hairs. There is no ring. A large, showy volva encloses the stem base. It is white to tan in color and its tissue is soft, delicate and easily torn.

| July | Aug. | Sept. |

Habitat

Amanita fulva is found in or near bogs and also in low damp areas of coniferous and deciduous woods.

Gills: crowded and free

Tawny Grisette

Note prominently grooved margin and lack of ring.

Cap: 1-3"

Stem: 3-4"

Typical Amanita trait; look for the large white volva.

Yellow Patches *Amanita flavoconia*

Decorative chrome-yellow patches on the yellow-orange cap make this an especially attractive mushroom. The cap is oval at first, then gradually becomes flatter with age. Cap surface is sticky when moist and the yellow patches are easily rubbed off. The margin may be faintly lined and hung with veil remnants. The thin cap flesh is white.

Moderately broad gills are free from the stem and set closely together. They are white with yellowish edges. A hand lens will reveal that they are fringed with tiny hairs.

The slender stem is white to pale yellow with a powdering of small wooly flakes on the surface. It tapers upward from its small bulb-like base. A persistent skirt-like ring hangs on the upper stem. The ring is white to yellowish with a yellow underside. The stem base has a covering of tattered, crumbling bits of yellow veil. These veil fragments are also buried in the soil. The stem tends to become hollow with age.

This is a common mushroom and often emerges during dry periods when other mushrooms fail to fruit.

Habitat
Under hardwoods and conifers, particularly Hemlock. Mycorrhizal.

◄ *Cap: 1-4"* ►

Stem: 2–4"

Spore Print

| July | Aug. | Sept. | Oct. |

Yellow Patches

Gills: crowded and free

The Blusher
Amanita rubescens

All parts of this common mushroom display dull red stains when bruised or cut. The dome-shaped cap of young specimens flattens with age.

There is a wide variation of cap color—rose-brown, buff, bronze, yellowish, olive or dark red-brown. All caps, when fresh, will display remnants of veil material in the form of grayish-pink, irregularly-shaped warts. These are randomly scattered on the cap, sometimes in dense clusters. Cap surface is tacky when moist.

The broad, crowded gills are free at maturity. Note the many shorter gills interspersed with regular gills. Gills are white, and soon become spotted with wine-red stains especially with handling.

The stout stem is club shaped with a rounded, swollen base. The stem is initially stuffed with fibers but becomes hollow with age. A pallid, membranous ring hangs on the upper stem. It is thin, fragile and skirt-like. Edges of the ring are often frayed and irregular.

Cleft-footed Amanita *Amanita brunnescens*

Habitat
Coniferous and deciduous woods, but especially under oak. Mycorrhizal.

Cap: 2–8"

The Blusher

Stem: 3–8"

| July | Aug. | Sept. | Oct. |

Spore Print

An easily embarrassed mushroom—The Blusher turns red if it's touched or bruised.

What makes this amanita distinctive is its bulbous "cleft foot" (the vertically-split stem base) and the dark, gray-brown cap. The cap is initially rounded, and then becomes flat with a broad, low central hump. Coloration at cap center is darker. Margins are lighter. The smooth cap surface is inlayed by darker fibers that create radial streaking. A scattering of whitish to tan felt-like patches adorn the cap. The surface is sticky during damp weather. The broad, cream-colored gills lining the cap underside are free and close. Gill edges are often scalloped.

The sturdy, white stem widens downward to a large, bulbous base. This bulb has a sharp, well-defined rim and is split vertically, usually in four places ("cleft-footed"). A membranous white ring hangs on the upper stem. It is often frayed and tattered and tends to collapse and adhere to the stem.

All parts of this mushroom stain reddish-brown when bruised or cut. The flesh may have a "raw potato" odor.

Habitat
Coniferous and deciduous woods, but especially under oak. Mycorrhizal.

Gills: crowded and free

Cap: 1-6"

Spore Print

Stem: 2–6"

Cleft-footed Amanita

Look for clefts in bulbous base.

| July | Aug. | Sept. | Oct. |

Why so Brittle?

All Russulas are characterized by a special brittleness. Mushrooms are composed of long cylindrical filaments called hyphae. These create a fibrous, reasonably sturdy tissue. Russula fruiting bodies have another component—large, thin-walled spherical cells called sphaerocysts. These cells mix with the hyphal filaments, often forming groupings like rosettes or islands in the mushroom tissue.

The round sphaerocysts are physically less stable than longer thread-like hyphae. Their considerable presence in Russula bodies makes the mushrooms vulnerable to snapping.

Field-testing for Russulas: If the mushroom's stem snaps crisply apart, you've got a Russula

Yellow Swamp Russula *Russula claroflava*

Let's start by saying up front that *Russula* identification is at best an iffy proposition. Even examined under a microscope, mycologists can't agree on species characteristics! That said, this mushroom has a bright, chrome-yellow to lemon-yellow cap, white to pale ochre gills and white stem. The stem develops noticeable gray to black areas as the mushroom ages. An important feature for identification is its tendency to very slowly turn gray and then black after it is cut or bruised. This color change can be seen in all parts. There are other yellow-capped russulas that turn gray to black when injured, but they do so very quickly. *Russula lutea*, another yellow-capped mushroom, does not show any color change when bruised and has a sticky cap.

Habitat
You find Yellow Swamp Russula in swampy woods (surprise!), and often under birch.

Spore Print

Gills: adnexed to almost free

This species has a dry yellow cap while the closely related species, Russula lutea, has a sticky yellow cap.

Cap: 2-4"

Stem: 2–3" tall

The flesh will slooowly turn gray and then black when bruised.

Yellow Swamp Russula

| July | Aug. | Sept. | Oct. |

Emetic Russula *Russula emetica*

This is a standout in the piney woods and sphagnum bogs where it appears. The mushroom cap is cherry to blood red.* Below are close, broad, white gills and a pure white stem. The cap may be somewhat slimy or sticky and the red may fade out in rain or with age. The whole mushroom body is so brittle that it easily breaks in your hand. Emetic Russula is not found in deciduous woods. The not-so-pleasant name, *Russula emetica*, suggests the mushroom's chemical make-up can cause vomiting *(emetic means "that which induces vomit")*.

Habitat
Solitary, scattered or in groups in woods. In sphagnum moss under conifers or in mixed woods. Rarely on rotten wood. Mycorrhizal.

Gills: nearly free and varied length

Spore Print

| July | Aug. | Sept. | Oct. |

Cap may be convex, flat or slightly depressed.

"Slippery when wet" cap dries to shiny red.

◀— Cap: 2-4" —▶

Flesh crumbles easily, like chalk.

Emetic Russula

Stem: 2–3"

*Note that there are many red-capped, white-stemmed Russulas in the woods.

Field and Lab

Russulas *can be relied upon to add color and interest to any North Woods trail walk from early summer to late fall. These common mushrooms are typically tidy in appearance with smooth, rounded to level caps, neat white gills and white cylindrical stems. The range of their cap colors is truly impressive, spanning the spectrum from white to red to purple-black to yellow.*

There are so many look-alike Russulas that, with a few exceptions, field identification is impossible. It takes study in the lab to verify their scientific names. There is one important feature that Russulas share; all have minute starchy ornamentation on the surface of their spores. Under a microscope these literally light up in blue when moistened by a drop of the iodine solution called Melzer's reagent. This so-called amyloid reaction is an important feature of the Russula.

Short-stalked White Russula *Russula brevipes* (formerly *Russula delica*)

The Short-stalked White Russula is a very common North Woods mushroom. It is often found at the edge of footpaths in pine needle duff and wood debris, its white cap barely emerging from the litter. In fact, it is often found by seeing a hump in the moss or duff of the forest floor—a "mushrump," if you will. When picked, dirt and needles cling to it, giving it a scruffy appearance. Once the dirt is removed, you have a very robust firm mushroom, creamy white overall.

The cap of this species is dry and made felty by a mat of tiny white fibrils. The smooth edges of the cap tend to turn down and with age the cap takes on a funnel shape. The thin gills are crowded under the cap and descend the stalk slightly. Take a careful look at the gills. Note that they are alternately long and short, that they fork and are joined by veins.

Unlike similar white *Lactarius* species (Milk Caps) (pg. 33), this mushroom does not exude latex.

Russula brevipes may be transformed into a completely different looking mushroom by the parasitic fungus, *Hypomyces lactifluorum* (nicknamed "The Lobster," see page 123), which engulfs the entire mushroom in a bright orange over coating.

Habitat
Scattered or in groups under conifers or mixed woods.

Like all Russulas, the flesh is very brittle and the stem can be snapped like a piece of chalk.

Cap: 4-8"

Stem: 1-3"

Gills: varied length and decurrent   *Spore Print*

Look for faint flush of blue-green where stem joins cap.

| July | Aug. | Sept. | Oct. |

Cap, gills and stem stain brown when cut or bruised.

Short-stalked White Russula

Blackening Russula *Russula dissimulans* group (formerly *Russula nigricans*)

This grayish-white *Russula* has a broadly-rounded cap that flattens with age and develops a shallow central depression. The margin is incurved at first. The cap has a smooth, dry surface and an interior of firm, white flesh which discolors to a grayish-rose when bruised or cut. The thick, closely-spaced gills may vary in color from cream to light straw-colored in gathered specimens. Note that many partial gills lay between gills of regular length. The mushroom's straight, thick stem is brittle and may be easily broken. Stem exterior is smooth and white.

Blackening?

Russula dissimulans belongs to a group of russulas that age and deteriorate in stages marked by color change. The flesh of the body reddens at first, then grays and finally, as it rots, turns brownish-black. In final stages of deterioration, these Blackening Russulas become habitat for small round-capped or puffball-like fungi called Powder Caps (see page 68)

Habitat

Growing singly or scattered in coniferous or oak woods. Mycorrhizal.

Cap: 2-8"

Stem: 1–3"

Spore Print

Blackening Russula

| June | July | Aug. | Sept. |

The Rooter (Rooted Collybia) *Xerula furfuracea (Oudemansiella radicata)*

A tall, attractive mushroom with a long rooting stem base. The cap is convex to flat with a distinct, central knob. The honey-colored to gray-brown surface has a thick, rather elastic skin (cuticle) that is sunken and wrinkled around the wide, rounded knob. The cap margin has a translucent quality. Broad, rounded, pure white gills are a bright contrast to the darker cap. Gills are attached initially but later cede and hang free. There is a mix of regular length and shorter gills.

The long, sturdy stem tapers upward. Stem may be somewhat twisted with longitudinal dark lines. Dig carefully to find its "root" extending down into the soil. *X. furfuracea* appears to be growing out of soil but may actually be fruiting on buried hardwood roots.

X. furfuracea is easily identified by its white spore print, slender stature and very distinctive long tapering "root" that extends well into the ground.

Habitat

Solitary, scattered or in groups on ground near old stumps or decaying deciduous logs, especially beech. Saprophytic.

Cap: ¹/₂–4"

Stem: 3–10"

Hard to miss: Note the unusually long, graceful, stem that tapers toward the top.

May	June	July	Aug.	Sept.	Oct.

The Rooter

Spore Print

Gills: varied length, well separated and free

False Chanterelle *Hygrophoropsis aurantiaca*

Bright orange gills and nicely uplifted margin make this an attractive find. The cap is flat, then funnel-shaped with an orange and brown color mix. The center is dark, the margin pale. The cap has a suede-like surface, especially over the center, and a thin, soft, white to orange-tinted flesh. Narrow, very crowded gills add a flashy touch of orange. They are repeatedly forked, blunt-edged in young specimens, but become blade-like as the fruiting body matures. There is an orange-brown, finely hairy stalk which is often off-center, sometimes nearly lateral. Stalk may be twisted and curved. It is enlarged at the base.

Cap: 1-3"

False Chanterelle

Stem: 1-4"

False Chanterelle: look for true, thin, blade-shaped gills.

Chanterelle look-alike?

Though called "False Chanterelle" because it vaguely resembles *Cantharellus cibarius* (Chanterelle pg. 81), a number of features help differentiate them. The egg-yolk yellow Chanterelle is NOT a true gilled mushroom, but rather has round-edged ridges or folds, set widely apart. It is also solid, more robust and fleshy.

H. aurantiaca is orange to orange-brown with soft, thin flesh and gills that are narrow, very crowded and, in mature specimens, blade-like. A fresh Chanterelle has a pleasant, fruity odor. *H. aurantiaca* does not.

Habitat

Found on the ground in pine needle duff and woody debris and on conifer logs and stumps.

Aug.	Sept.	Oct.	Nov.

Gills: narrow, crowded and decurrent

Spore Print

Latin vs. Common

Names of mushrooms can be a bit confusing at times. Some fungi are known only by their scientific name while others are known by one or more common names (which vary from region to region). Roughly, the names can be put into three categories. First are those that possess an established common name. These include Alcohol Inky, Shaggy Mane, Chanterelle, Old Man of the Woods, Honey Mushroom, and Morel. Each of these has a scientific name, but is usually called by its common name.

Secondly are those that incorporate the scientific name as part of the common name. Examples of these are: Amanita, Russula and Cortinarius (Corts).

Finally, many are known only by their scientific names. Some genera with this status are Pluteus, Clitocybe, Laccaria, Panaeolus, Xeromphalina *and* Entoloma.

Unfortunately, many of the scientific names are in flux and taxonomic changes occur regularly. What we try to do in this book is to use the accepted common names and the most recent scientific names. Whatever the name, fungi are fascinating to look at and fun getting to know. Good luck!

The Gypsy *Rozites caperata*

Look for the silver-violet glaze covering the center of the cap, a feature that sets the Gypsy apart from look-a-likes. This silvery coating is notable on young emerging fruiting bodies and persists to maturity.

The Gypsy is a neatly proportioned mushroom with an orange-brown cap, wrinkled on top and puckering at the margin. At maturity the cap is rounded to flat with a broad central hump.

Flesh of the cap is thick and white.

The gills are close, broad, and off-white. They are attached to a solid white stem. A thick, persistent yellowish ring hangs mid-way on the stem.

← *Cap: 2-6"*

CHOICE

The Gypsy

Stem: 2–5"

Habitat
Single to scattered groups in pine, fir and hardwood stands. Mycorrhizal.

Spore Print

July	Aug.	Sept.	Oct.

Sphagnum-bog Galerina

For those brave enough to saunter through the sodden sphagnum moss of a Black Spruce/Tamarack bog in early summer, a delicate fungal treat awaits. *Galerina paludosa* peaks proudly above the deep sphagnum hummocks.

← *Cap: ³/₈–1¹/₈"*

Sphagnum-bog Galerina

Stem: 2–4"

Galerina paludosa

Wet knees are required to see its distinctly banded stem. From above, the dark-nippled cap gives it away. Very common in this uncommonly visited habitat.

Habitat
Mossy mature Black Spruce/ Tamarack bogs with fairly closed canopy.

Gills: narrow, crowded and decurrent

Spore Print

| July | Aug. | Sept. | Oct. |

Straw-colored Fiberhead *Inocybe fastigiata*

A peaked straw hat with up-turned brim is what the cap of this mushroom resembles.

It is yellow-brown to dark honey-brown and its surface is thickly covered with fine fibers. These are light and dark in tone and lie radially, giving the cap a streaked appearance. When young, the cap is bell-shaped, but as the cap expands it becomes flatter with a cone-shaped hump and a flared, splitting margin. Cap flesh is thin and white, yellowing as the mushroom matures. When wet, the surface of the cap is slippery. The mushroom's close-set, narrow gills are white with an olive tint.

Edges are paler. At maturity gills color to coffee-brown. The white to ochre stem widens downward, but there is no basal bulb. It is lined longitudinally, and often twisted. Its surface is made smooth and silky by a coat of delicate hairs.

An odor of green corn may be noted in some specimens.

Habitat
In moss under conifer and hardwood. In grassy openings, pastures. Mycorrhizal.

Cap: ¾–3½"

Stem: 1½–3½"

| May | June |

Straw-colored Fiberhead

Spore Print

Gills: narrow, close-set

Poison Pax *Paxillus involutus*

A very common mushroom of compact build with a stem usually shorter in height than the width of the cap. The dingy yellowish-brown cap is covered with soft, matted hairs and there may be a hint of zoning or spotting on the surface. The cap center is depressed and the margin is strongly inrolled on young specimens, cracking with age. The rim may be ribbed and have a cottony coating.

Tightly-packed ochre gills have conspicuous cross veins and forking and are often pore-like close to the stem. Note that pressure with your thumb will easily loosen the gills from the cap.

The short, sturdy stem is colored much like the cap. It may be attached at the cap center or slightly to the side. It is frequently tapered downward. The surface of the stem is smooth. There is no ring.

All parts of this mushroom stain brown to reddish-brown when cut or bruised.

Cap: 3/4–3 1/2"

Poison Pax

Poison Pax is poisonous

Though this mushroom has long been eaten in Europe, it is now known to be poisonous. It must never be eaten raw, and even when cooked there is danger. Studies have revealed that consumption of this mushroom over a period of years may have serious and often deadly consequences. Due to a hyper-allergic reaction, the body gradually produces anti-bodies which destroy red blood cells. This process, called hemolysis, results in extreme anemia and can lead to kidney failure.

Poison Pax darkens brown to reddish-brown when bruised

Habitat

On the ground or on decaying wood in coniferous and mixed woodlands. It also appears on lawns and in bogs. Mycorrhizal.

Stem: 1 1/2–3 1/2"

Gills: decurrent and closely spaced

Spore Print

| June | July | Aug. | Sept. | Oct. |

Canary Trich *Tricholoma flavovirens*

When young and fresh, the vivid yellow cap of this mushroom contrasts with the bed of rust-brown needle duff where it fruits. The cap is rounded at first becoming flatter with a wide, low umbo as it ages. The margin of mature caps is often curled and uplifted, and may be split. The smooth, even cap surface tends to be slimy to tacky. Dominant cap color is bright yellow, but fine scaling adds definite tints of olive-brown or reddish-brown over the cap center. No dark, radially arranged fibers will be present on the cap surface. Flesh of the cap is white, firm and thick with a thin layer of pale yellow just below the cuticle.

The gills are sulfur-yellow, broad and fairly close. They are notched at the stem and often of uneven lengths. Gill edges become ragged and wavy as the mushroom matures.

Cap: 1–2½"

The stout, solid stem is cylindrical but, at times, with a bulbous base. Stems of older specimens may be hollow. The pale-yellow to sulfur-yellow stem surface is smooth, dry, and usually hairless. Olive or yellow-brown stains may be found on the lower stem and stem base.

Specimens often have an odor similar to that of fresh meal.

Habitat
Under pine in sandy soils. Mycorrhizal.

Aug.	Sept.	Oct.	Nov.

Stem: 2–4"

Canary Trich

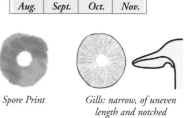

Spore Print

Gills: narrow, of uneven length and notched

Amethyst Laccaria *Laccaria amethystina*

Bright purple cap, gills and stem distinguish this small gem-like mushroom of mossy, moist-soiled hardwood forests. The broadly rounded cap has a wavy, often in-rolled margin. There is a central depression. The surface is smooth for the most part, though with age the cap center may break into tiny, soft scales. The cap tends to hold moisture and, when fresh, has a somewhat translucent quality. As the mushroom matures its color fades to light brownish-purple. Color of the cap flesh is pale lilac.

The waxy deep-purple gills are thick, moderately broad and widely-spaced. They are attached to the stem and extend downward.

The purple stem is elastic yet tough, and becomes hollow by maturity. Its surface is coarsely hairy or scaly, particularly midway down the stem. Its base is coated with white or lilac mycelium. The mushroom has a faint fruity odor.

Habitat

Scattered or in groups in shady hardwood forests, especially under oak and beech. Mycorrhizal.

Cap: ³/8–2"

Stem: ³/8–3"

Amethyst Laccaria

Spore Print

| July | Aug. | Sept. |

Bog Laccaria

A long stem allows this small mushroom to rise above the thick sphagnum and makes it visible to the mushroom hunter. Its orange-brown cap is broadly rounded with a shallow central depression. The thin margin is striate, somewhat translucent and often upturned. When fresh, the smooth to finely hairy cap surface is moist or oily

Cap: ³/8–3"

Bog Laccaria

Stem: 2¹/2–6¹/2"

| Aug. | Sept. | Oct. |

Laccaria longipes

to the touch. Pale pinkish gills are attached, broad and widely set.

Spore Print

The length of its slender stem helps distinguish this mushroom from closely related species. The stem is cylindrical with a dry, lined surface. Its base is somewhat swollen and covered with white mycelium. The stem, like the cap, is orange-brown.

Habitat

Found in sphagnum moss under conifers. Mycorrhizal and saprophytic.

Gills: varied length and adnate

Club Foot *Clitocybe clavipes*

Clusters and rings of this mushroom are a common find, especially under Eastern White Pine. A large, swollen stem base is the mushroom's most obvious feature and inspires its common name, Club Foot. The mature cap is flat with a shallow, central depression. Its margin is thin, down-turned and sometimes wavy. Cap color may be yellowish-buff, gray-brown or olive brown. The margin is paler. The center of the smooth, moist cap is often made felty by a cover of fine fibers. Pale-yellow gills line the cap underside. Their color fades with age. These are fairly wide-set and may vary from narrow to broad. Cross veins and forking can be noted. Gills are deeply decurrent.

The whitish stem widens downward into a greatly enlarged base. Its surface is darkened by vertical streaks of olive-tinted fibers. The swollen base is soft and spongy, but tough. Under extremely dry conditions it will become brittle. A cottony mycelium surrounds the base.

Specimens may have a sweet, fruity scent.

Habitat

Found under conifers and in mixed woods, especially under Eastern White Pine. Mycorrhizal.

Cap: ³/4–2¹/2"

Eating this mushroom when alcohol has recently been consumed can cause headache, rash and flushing.

Stem: 2¹/2–2¹/2"

Spore Print

July	Aug.	Sept.	Oct.	Nov.

Club Foot

Forest Funnel Cap *Clitocybe gibba*

When mature, this tidy, pinkish-tan mushroom with its smooth pale stem suggests a small wine cup. The cap becomes deeply depressed, almost funnel-shaped. The gills that line the underside of the up-turned cap are crowded, white, descending a short way onto the stalk. This mushroom often appears in early summer before other gilled mushrooms make their appearance.

Habitat
Solitary and in groups in decaying leaves, especially under oak. Saprophytic.

Gills: varied length and decurrent   *Spore Print*

Like some other mushrooms and plants, C. gibba releases minute amounts hydrogen cyanide into the atmosphere.

← Cap: 2-3" →

Stem:
1–3¼"

Base often with cottony mycelial growth.

July	Aug.	Sept.	Oct.

Leaf litter adheres to the stem base.

Funnel Cap

The Miller *Clitopilus prunulus*

This mushroom is said to have an odor like fresh ground meal and so is commonly called "The Miller." The dull white to grayish cap is irregular

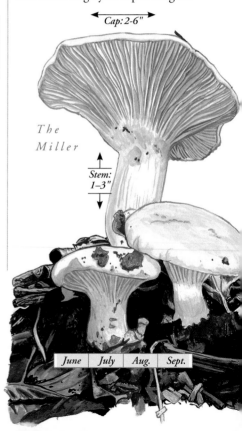

← Cap: 2-6" →

The Miller

Stem:
1–3"

June	July	Aug.	Sept.

in shape with a sunken center and an inrolled margin that becomes flaring, lobed and wavy with age. The cap surface is suede-like. The flesh is white and firm. The gills are fairly well-spaced and descend deeply down the stalk. Gills are white, but once the spores mature, they take on a pinkish hue. The stalk, colored like the cap, has a dry, somewhat cottony surface. It is vertically ridged and often has a swollen mid-section. It is typically off-center.

Habitat

The Miller fruits alone or in scattered groupings in grassy areas in open woodlands. It is frequently found under juniper. May grow from rotting boards on buildings.

Spore Print

Gills: decurrent and closely spaced

Wine-cap Stropharia *Stropharia rugosoannulata*

Large maroon-red to chestnut-brown cap, wide, violet-tinted gills and a white stem with a unique ring, make this mushroom eye-catching. The cap presents a dry smooth surface. With age, cracks may develop on the surface and the margin often splits. Whitish at first, the gills later take on a violet-gray color and finally become brownish-black when the mature spores are released.

The firm, smooth stem has a bulbous base surrounded by white mycelial threads. In very wet weather, the stem wall may break to form curls of stem tissue. The stem has a telling feature: a large, thick, membranous ring, grooved along its upper rim. The lower section of the ring is separated into claw-like points.

This mushroom is easy to cultivate in straw or on wood chips. Masses of mushroom mycelium are developed

Cap: 2-6"

Stem: 4-6"

| June | July | Aug. | Sept. | Oct. |

Wine-cap Stropharia

The stalk holds a partial white veil that leaves a persistent membranous ring with claw-like points.

commercially and made available to growers.

Habitat

Scattered to numerous on wood chips, mulch, straw, gardens, lawns or cultivated fields. Saprophytic.

Spore Print

Gills: adnate and closely spaced

Milky Mystery

How is it that a mushroom exudes "milk?" A number of mushrooms, particularly those commonly known as Milk Caps (Lactarius), have specialized hyphae called lactifers. These large tubular structures store the thick fluid that oozes out when the flesh of those mushrooms is cut or injured. In Lactarius, the tubular milk-storing hyphae are long

and have numerous branches that end in the tissues near the outer surface. When you cut them, they readily produce the "bleeding" effect. The fluid (latex) can be colorless or variously colored: blue, red, orange, yellow or white.

Saffron Milk Cap *Lactarius deliciosus*

This sturdy mushroom with a green-staining orange cap is found in coniferous woods, especially under pines. The cap is flat, centrally depressed and has an inrolled margin. Its surface, when young, is covered with a whitish bloom. It is typically shiny and somewhat sticky and is decorated by concentrically arranged salmon-orange to purple spots and streaks. Gills are pale-orange, narrow and crowded with some cross veins and forking. They often show greenish stains.

The firm stem is cylindrical, becoming hollow with age. Its surface is smooth or may have a series of spot-like depressions. Mycelium may be found at the stem base.

All parts of this mushroom stain green when injured; even the orange latex turns green when exposed to the air. You may detect a fruity odor.

Habitat
Single to scattered to gregarious in moist areas, boggy places, along streams, under conifers; especially pine. Mycorrhizal.

Spore Print

Saffron Milk Cap

Cap: 2-5"

Stem: 1–3"

| July | Aug. | Sept. | Oct. |

Flesh stains green when bruised. Exudes orange latex when cut.

Note whitish bloom on young caps.

Gills: decurrent and closely spaced

Indigo Milk Cap *Lactarius indigo*

If color could define a living thing, "blue" would define this milk cap mushroom. The cap, gills and stem of a fresh young specimen are indigo. The broad cap is depressed at the center and

Cap: 2-6"

Indigo Milk Cap

Stem: 1–3¹/₂"

Indigo-blue latex is exuded when any part is cut.

Note decurrent gills.

has a thick inrolled margin. The surface is smooth, sticky, and decorated with concentric zones of deep blue. Cap flesh is brittle, pallid with a bluish tint. As the mushroom matures, the cap color fades to a lustrous blue-gray. The deep blue, attached gills are set close together and descend the stem slightly. The rigid stem is blue to silvery blue-gray, cylindrical, hard and hollow. All parts of the mushroom stain blue-green when bruised.

Habitat
Scattered or in groups on soil in oak and pine woods.

July	Aug.	Sept.	Oct.

Spore Print

Gills: closely spaced

Pepper Milk Cap
Lactarius piperatus

Like others in its genus, this large cream-colored mushroom exudes a fluid (latex) when cap or gills are cut. Pepper Milk Cap has a dull, dry cap with hairless margin. The gills are extremely crowded with numerous forkings. The latex is white, sharply bitter and very hot to taste.

Habitat
Scattered to grouped on soil in deciduous woods; some in mixed forests. Mycorrhizal.

Spore Print

Gills: decurrent and closely spaced

Cap: 3-10"

Pepper Milk Cap

Stem: 1"

July	Aug.	Sept.

Burnt Sugar Milk Cap *Lactarius aquifluus (L. helvus)*

A pleasing scent of burnt sugar or curry is notable in this sturdy mushroom. It can be numerous at the edges of sphagnum bogs. The rounded cap is light cinnamon-brown to fawn-colored with hints of pink. Cap margin is inrolled at first. Mature specimens develop a flatter cap, sometimes with a central depression. The smooth cap surface is blanketed with white silky fibers which eventually become scale-like. Dark water spots may be present on the surface. When cut, the cap releases a watery, colorless latex. The pale, pinkish-brown gills are crowded under the cap. They are attached and may descend a short way down the stem. Gills are broad in mature specimens, forking near the stem, and darken with age.

The rather slender stem is often hollow. Its surface has a whitish downy or powdery bloom. White mycelial threads cover the stem base.

Fungal Air Freshener
The burnt sugar odor is persistent and strong, and grows more evident when the mushroom dries. Placing one on your car's dashboard, or in some enclosed spot, will nicely scent the air.

Habitat
In sphagnum bogs and low forested lands with conifers. Mycorrhizal.

Cap: 2-3"

Stem: 1–3 1/2"

| July | Aug. | Sept. | Oct. |

Gills: adnate to slightly decurrent and closely spaced

Spore Print

Burnt Sugar Milk Cap

Bracelet Cort (Banded Cort) *Cortinarius armillatus*

The red banded stem ("bracelet") makes this mushroom easy to recognize. It is a medium to large mushroom, quite robust and impressive in stature.

Cap: 2-6"

Look for several uneven, red, concentric bands circling the stem.

Bracelet Cort

Stem: 2–6"

The tawny-brown to reddish-brown cap is initially bell-shaped, but with maturity, it becomes flatter, often with a broad central hump and down-turned margin. Its dry surface has a covering of delicate hairs and may, as it ages, develop soft scales. White veil remnants often cling to the cap edge. Cap flesh is cream to buff in color. Young gills are a pale brown and later turn rust-brown. They are broad, well-spaced and

attached to the stem or notched just before the stem. Gill edges may be scalloped and lighter in color.

The stem is thick and dry with club-shaped or bulbous base. The stem surface has scatterings of silky, reddish hairs. A zone of white fibers can be seen at the top of the stem. Below, two to four broad bands of dull-red veil tissue circle the stem. Flesh of the stem is darker than that of the cap.

The mushroom may have a slight radish-like odor.

Habitat
Under birch and pine. Mycorrhizal.

Spore Print

Gills: notched and attached

| Aug. | Sept. | Oct. |

Violet Cort (Purple Cort) *Cortinarius violaceus*

An exceptional woodland beauty with deep violet cap, gills and stem. Flesh is blue to deep purple. The cap becomes flattened with a low central

Spore Print

hump and is densely covered with fibrous, violet scales. The broad gills are widely spaced and eventually take on a rusty-brown tone as spores are released. The cortina is a cobwebby partial veil that is present under the cap (see inset on next page). The stem widens toward a rounded base.

The uniform dark-violet color and dry scaly cap help set this mushroom apart from others with violet coloring. It is not, in spite of its color, a good source of fiber dye.

Cortinarius is a very large genus and may have 1000 members in North America.

Habitat

Solitary, scattered, or in groups among mosses under conifers or mixed woods: fir, pine, aspen, alder, oak. May be near decomposed logs. Mycorrhizal with conifers and deciduous trees.

Violet Cort

Note the fibrous scales on the cap that separate this species from the few other blue and purple mushrooms in the North Woods.

Cap: 2–4¾"

Stem: 3–7"

| Sept. | Oct. |

Gills: free and closely spaced

Spotted Cort

Violet is the color theme carried out in the cap, gills, stem and flesh of this mushroom. The broadly-rounded cap is smooth and decidedly slimy when wet. It has a splattering of pale yellow spots on an otherwise violet surface. The violet gills are attached, close and

Cap and stem slimy when wet.

Cap: 1-2"

The stem is often bulbous at the base.

Stem: 2-3"

| July | Aug. | Sept. |

Spotted Cort

Cortinarius iodes

quite broad. As the mushroom matures, the gills take on a cinnamon-gray coloration due to the release of rusty-brown spores. The smooth, solid stem is, like the cap, very slimy when wet. Cobwebby veil remnants ring the upper stem. Both stem and veil are violet.

The mushroom has a pleasant odor.

Habitat

Look for Spotted Cort growing singly or in groups, on the ground under deciduous trees.

Gills: adnate and closely spaced

Spore Print

Rimmed-bulb Cort group *Cortinarius* species

This mushroom belongs to a group of yellowish to orange *Cortinarius* species with an abrupt rim on the bulbous stems. Its thick, firm cap is rounded with an incurved margin. It becomes flatter with age. The cap surface is slimy when moist. The coloration of the cap varies from all yellow to ochre to orange with a yellowish margin and there are sometimes spot-like surface scales. The flesh has a radish-like odor. Yellow to ochre gills are set close together. They are attached and may be notched at the

Veil remnants *Incurved margin*

Note the incurved margin, the veil remnants and how the close-set gills attach to the stem—common traits of young Corts.

stem. Eventually, gills are tinted rusty-brown by mature spores. The stout, solid stem is short with a large rimmed bulbous base. The rim is most distinct in young specimens.

Habitat

This is a widely distributed group of species that grows singly or in groups on the ground under hardwoods or conifers.

Cap: 2-5"

Rimmed-bulb Cort

Stem: 1–2"

| June | July | Aug. |

Spore Print

Gills: adnate and closely spaced

Capturing a Mushroom's Color

Beautiful colors can be extracted from fungi...but not necessarily the color of the mushroom. Because some species may be poisonous, preparation of the dyes needs to be done away from the kitchen. In one large pot (not aluminum), 2-3 quarts of water and 10 grams of alum are heated. The yarns or other fibers are put into the hot (not boiling) water and set aside for one hour. Meanwhile the mushrooms (about a quart) are boiled in 2-3 quarts of water for one hour, then allowed to cool slightly. The yarns/fibers are then carefully drained and placed in the hot mushroom liquid together with the mushrooms. Steep one hour, stirring occasionally. Yarns/fibers are then carefully rinsed. Add one cup of vinegar to one rinse. Give the material a final rinse and hang to dry out of the direct sun. Get out your knitting needles!

Red-gilled Cort *Cortinarius semisanguineus*

The yellow-brown fibrous cap is quite ordinary. At first, it is bell shaped. The mature cap is flat with a slightly raised center called an umbo. When the dull cap is turned over, however, there is a surprise. The gill-bearing underside sports a startling, blood-red or cinnabar coloration. The red gills are closely packed, narrow and broadly attached to the mushroom's yellow stem. The stem is pale at the top and reddish at its base. Since this is a *Cortinarius* species, its developing gills had been protected with a web-like covering called a cortina. The remnants of that covering form a fibrous zone on the upper stalk. You may notice a slight odor of radish when handling this fungus.

Note the distinctive reddish-colored gills.

Can be found late into autumn; even fruiting in November.

Habitat
The mushroom can be found in moist mixed-forest depressions where sphagnum and other mosses have taken hold. It likes the company of a tangle of blueberry shrubs.

◄— Cap: 1-2" —►

Stem: 4"

Red-gilled Cort

Dyeing Breed

C. semisanguineus has a proven track record as a source of fiber dye. When cooked with alum as mordant it yields a yellow to red dye. A warm cinnamon-orange color is achieved when the dye is applied to various fibers including wool. Attaining dyes from mushroom species has a long history and is becoming a popular interest and occupation today. There are international fungus-fiber symposiums held a various cities around the world. In their book, *Rainbow at My Feet*, mushroom experts, Arlene and Alan Bessette explore the many facets of this fascinating subject. [See sidebar on previous page]

Gills: adnate and closely spaced

Spore Print

Aug.	Sept.	Oct.	Nov.

Witch's Hat *Hygrophorus conicus*

This mushroom's conical hat with pointed central peak earns it the common name Witch's Hat. The cap may be variously colored: bright red, red-orange or yellow with hints of green. It is thin, fragile and translucent with a smooth surface. When moist, it is somewhat sticky. The cap edge is striate and often splits as the fruiting body matures. The closely spaced yellow gills are thick, soft and waxy. They eventually become torn and unevenly frayed.

There is a delicate cylindrical stem that is colored like the cap. It may be twisted and longitudinally lined. White mycelium can be seen at the stem base.

A telling characteristic of this fungus is that it blackens readily when bruised and becomes blackened with age.

Habitat

It fruits under conifers and is very common.

Cap: 2-4"

Spore Print

Stem: 3–6"

Note longitudinal lines on stem.

Witch's Hat

All of the Witch's Hat will blacken when bruised. You may find an all black one in the field.

June	July	Aug.	Sept.

Gills: free and well spaced

Scarlet Waxy Cap *Hygrophorus coccineus*

The form and color of this mushroom are captivating. The cap is bell-shaped early on, then flat with a central depression, and often with a widely flaring margin. The surface is an intense scarlet with some yellow tints. The flesh is fragile and yellow-orange. The waxy gills (rub them between your fingers to feel the waxiness) curve broadly under the cap then descend the stalk a short way. Their color is red to orange-cream. There are numerous cross veins. The hollow

Cap: 1-4"

Stem: 1–3¹/₄"

The name "waxy cap" refers to the waxy texture of the flesh if rubbed between the fingers. Hygrophorus means "bearer of moisture."

stalk is red with a yellow base, often curved and flattened. It grows in dense clusters—often so crowded that the caps of some individuals are deformed from pressing up against their neighbor.

Specimens of *coccineus* tend to have an appealing originality about them: the tilt of cap, curve of gill, their variability and glow of color. They

are a favorite of photographers. Peaked red-orange caps appear greasy and are in fact moist to the touch.

Habitat

Scarlet Waxy Caps often appear in large groups in cool moist woods. Also in depressions dominated by balsam, hemlock and pine. Sometimes in grassy areas, clearings, meadows and often associated with mosses.

Scarlet Waxy Cap

| July | Aug. | Sept. | Oct. |

Gills appear as long triangles.

Note hollow stem.

Spore Print

Gills: well-separated and adnexed to free

Cap: 1-3"

Stem: 2–6"

White Waxy Cap

*Cap and stem are **very** slimy when wet.*

White (Ivory) Waxy Cap *Hygrophorus eburneus*

The soft–fleshed cap is flat with an incurved margin. As the mushroom matures the margin tips upward. The cap is smooth and bright white.

The white gills are well spaced and waxen and may bruise yellow. The slender stem is smooth, white and narrows downward to the base. In some specimens you may detect a strong odor of sage.

The most distinctive feature of *Hygrophorus ebruneus* is its very slimy cap and stem. White Waxy Cap is, as mycologist David Arora aptly puts it, the "slipperiest and slimiest gilled fungus among us."

Habitat
Single to scattered to gregarious on leaf litter of deciduous woods and grassy areas. May also appear in pine-oak, pine-beech woods. Appears to be mycorrhizal with beech on fertile soil.

Spore Print

Gills: decurrent and well-separated

Aug.	Sept.	Oct.	Nov.

Parrot Waxy Cap
Hygrophorus psittacina

The parrot mushroom is one of the gems of moist, mossy woodlands, catching filtered sunlight in its colorful translucent cap and stem. It begins with a bright green bell-shaped cap, green gills and stem. As it matures, a variety of lovely pastels intermingle with the green tones. If you take one in your hand, you will be amazed at the range of colors, all highlighted by the thin waxen flesh of the mushroom. It is uniquely beautiful.

Parrot Waxy Cap

Cap: 3/8–1 1/2"

Stem: 1 1/2–2 1/2"

Gills: Attached

July	Aug.	Sept.	Oct.

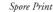

Spore Print

Alcohol Inky (Tippler's Bane) *Coprinus atramentarius*

Tight crowds of these glossy, lead-gray mushrooms appear in gardens, on stumps and in grassy places enriched by buried woody debris. Young caps are egg-shaped with margins puckered and pressed against the stem. At maturity, the mushrooms are bell-shaped with a grooved, splitting margin. Cap flesh is thin and pallid. The gills are set close together, broad and initially white in color but turning dark. The cylindrical, silky-white stem is hollow. A dark zone of veil material rings the lower stem.

Self Digestion

Coprinus species share a unique method of dispersing their spores. The self digestion process progresses from the margin to the stem, freeing the mature black spores. Left behind is a forlorn bunch of stems and a twisted, sheeting of inky, oil-like material.

Cap: 1 1/2–3"

Alcohol Inky

Stem: 1 1/2–6"

One of the earliest gilled fungi of the season.

May	June	July	Aug.	Sept.	Oct.

Booby Trap

Mycologist Bryce Kendrick calls *C. atramentarius* a "booby trap for drinkers." Coprine is a unique amino acid contained in this fungus. It is not itself a poison, but it causes considerable problems for anyone who consumes an alcoholic beverage within 48 to 96 hours of eating the mushroom. The unfortunate drinker will face an onset of alarming symptoms—flushing of face and neck, swelling and numbness of hands and face, rapid heartbeat, tingling extremities, nausea and vomiting. Coprine, which persists a long time in the diner's system after eating, blocks the body's metabolism of ethyl alcohol,

Coprinus mushrooms begin dissolving from the margin.

Note the dark zone of veil material

stopping the process at the acetaldehyde stage. Acetaldehyde is the poison causing the symptoms. It should be noted that the symptoms of coprine poisoning disappear on their own without treatment.

Habitat

Clustered in grasses and woody debris and near buried wood in lawns. Found in wood chips, decaying deciduous stumps, bases of unhealthy trees, especially aspen and poplar, in parks, gardens, along streets, residential areas and city dumps.

"Autodeliquescence:" these inky caps will soon be liquid. This liquid was once used for writing ink!

Gills: free and closely spaced

Spore Print

Shaggy Mane *Coprinus comatus*

The cap of the young mushroom is tall, column-like to oval with a smooth, white to ochre surface and a margin that is pressed in against the stem. The maturing mushroom expands to become bell-shaped. Its margin is lined and tattered. The cap's white outer skin (cuticle) breaks into broad, overlapping scales. Scale edges tend to fray and curl upward giving the mushroom a distinctive "shaggy dog" appearance. White gills are densely packed under the cap. They are free, straight and narrow. There is often a delicate pinkish tint in the gills. The silky, white stem is cylindrical and hollow.

There is a thin, movable ring low on the stem. The base of the stem is enlarged, pointed and rooting. Like other inky caps, Shaggy Mane disperses its spores by a gradual dissolving of cap and gill tissue. This is an easily recognized species with its column-like form and copiously scaly cap.

It is a much sought-after and choice edible. There are no toxic look-alikes.

Shaggy Mane

CHOICE

Habitat

Solitary, scattered or clustered in grass, wood chips, hard packed soil, along roads and trails as well as disturbed sites: lawns, pastures, gardens, garbage dumps, compost heaps. May grow in urban or suburban settings. Saprophytic.

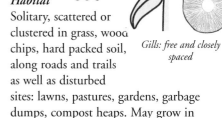

Gills: free and closely spaced

Cap: 1 1/4–3 1/4"

Cap: up to 6"

Scaly cap surface helps distinguish this species from the Alcohol Inky.

Strong? They've been known to push up through asphalt.

Stem: 2 1/2–8"

Spores black; but nearly impossible to get a print without a black gooey mess.

| June | July | Aug. | Sept. | Oct. |

Fairy Rings

Mushrooms drop their spores in a circular pattern and the resulting hungry hyphae expand outward, seeking nutrition. Your lawn is literally an even playing field; a substrate evenly composed of a constant and uninterrupted food supply. The "ring" of advancing mycelium expands like a ripple in a pool, finding and feasting on untapped organic matter in the soil. Depending on conditions, these rings will continue to expand, growing in circumference a few inches or a few feet every year. If the mycelium "decides" to produce fruiting bodies, the result is a fairy ring, popping up as a ring of mushrooms above the leading edge of the mycelia. The best known fairy ring mushroom is the edible Marasmius oreades (pg. 44), but several others, such as the Meadow Mushroom (Agaricus campestris), also follow this growth pattern.

Meadow Mushroom *Agaricus campestris*

Cap: 1½–4"

Stem: 1–2½"

CHOICE

Meadow Mushroom

Spore Print

These white-capped mushrooms appear in arcs, fairy rings or scattered groups on lawns, in meadows and pastures and along grassy roadsides. The smooth cap is typically dome-shaped, becoming flatter with age. The cap's center (disk) is often darkened by soft, gray-brown hairs or scales. These are especially evident during dry periods. The cap has thick, firm flesh that, at times, may be flushed with pinkish or brown tints. It does not stain when bruised. Look for frayed veil remnants; they're often found hanging from the strongly down-turned cap. Gills are free, narrow and crowded. Delicate young pink gills are a notable feature of this mushroom. As the mushroom expands, the gills become bright pink and eventually, with spore release, become chocolate-brown. The solid stem is short, giving the mushroom a squat appearance. The stem is dry and smooth above a narrow flimsy ring (ring often wears away). The stem surface below the ring is covered with fine fibers. Stem is white but becomes dingy reddish brown with age. There is no cup (volva) at the base. They tend to be abundant following rains and cool weather.

Supermarket Fare

Most shoppers are familiar with the typical white, fleshy mushroom sold in supermarkets. This commercially-grown mushroom is *Agaricus bisporus*, a very close relative of the Meadow Mushroom. The difference is microscopic, resting on the number of spores found on each spore producing basidia. In the case of *A. bisporus*, there are two spores per basidia; *A. campestris* usually has four spores. A bit of trivia for the common man, but important for separating the species in the lab.

Habitat

Solitary or in groups; often in fairy rings on the ground in grassy areas such as lawns, meadows, pastures, cemeteries, golf courses, parks and roadsides. Saprophytic.

Aug.	Sept.	Oct.

Gills: free and closely spaced

Spore Print

Shaggy Parasol *Lepiota rachodes*

A striking feature of this mushroom is the pattern of scales on its cap. The cap of the developing mushroom is pinkish to cinnamon-brown. As the cap grows and expands, the outer colored skin breaks into concentric circles of rough, curling tissues revealing the underlying pale surface. The mushroom body is large, with a thick, wide cap, broad whitish gills and a sturdy stalk with rounded base. If you cut away the cap you will see the upper portion of the stalk is hollow. The thick white ring on the upper stalk is membranous and moveable.

Ring edges may be reddish-brown. The cap and stem stain yellow-orange when cut.

Habitat

Can be found singly or sometimes in fairy ring groupings in grass along roads, on wood chips and on cultivated soils.

Cap: 2 1/8–8"

Stem: 4–8"

Note moveable, thick white annulus.

Gills: free and closely spaced

Shaggy Parasol

Spore Print

Aug.	Sept.	Oct.

Blewit *Lepista nuda (Clitocybe nuda)*

Look for a generous, late-fall fruiting of *C. nuda* on damp decaying leaf piles and compost heaps. The large mounds of organic material and soil pushed to the side of shady country roads by graders are also a likely place to find groups of fruiting bodies. Color is a defining feature; the cap, stalk and gills of young specimens are a clear lilac-blue. The thick-fleshed caps have a smooth, oily surface. Mature caps are flattened, often with a shallow central depression. They may develop cracks in dry weather. Eventually the caps take on a red-brown color and the thin cap margin, inrolled at first, tends to become uplifted, flared and wavy giving the mushroom a lopsided, jaunty look. Perhaps this inspired its common name Blewit (Blue Hat). Gills are broad and fade with age from lilac to pinkish-tan. They never, however, take on a rust color as do some other fungi with violet coloration. There is no veil. The Blewit's stem is solid and fibrous, often with a bulbous base. The base may be overlaid with whitish hairs and develop a brownish surface. You can frequently find a downy mat of violet-colored mycelium attached to the base. The mushroom has a fragrant odor of anise.

The Blewit seems to favor cool weather and tends to grow back when cut down. Due to the blue or violet cap, it may be confused with *Cortinarius*, but it doesn't have the latter's webby veil or spore color.

Habitat
Single to numerous on needle duff or leaf litter under conifers or hardwoods. Also in humus-rich ground, around sawdust, mounds of leaves, decomposing organic matter, even may grow on shredded newspaper. Also seen along paths and woods edges, beneath blackberry stems. May form fairy rings. Saprophytic.

Cap: 2-6"

Blewit in its prime

Blewit past prime

Stem: 1-3"

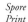

Blewit

| Aug. | Sept. | Oct. | Nov. |

Spore Print

Gills: adnate, closely spaced and sometimes notched

The FUNGI of LATE FALL & WINTER

October is a terrific time to hike the forests of the North Woods. Colorful leaves of red, orange and yellow put on a splendid display but while looking up at the leaves don't forget to look down for fall fungi.

Some of our yards may hold growths of Shaggy Mane and Alcohol Inkies or Meadow Mushrooms. If the Meadow Mushrooms look familiar, it may be because they are closely related to the cultivated ones we put on our pizzas and in our salads. Watch also for mature Puffballs whose golfball-like crusty exterior can be tapped to release a green cloud of millions of spores. Whether child or adult, it is hard not to step on these brown fungi just to see the tiny smoke signals. We may think stomping puffballs is hurting them, but we are actually helping them by dispersing their spores. Also out are the Giant Puffballs that may become the size of a deflated basketball.

But it is in the woods that the biggest growths of October mushrooms occur. At the base of dead oaks, maples or birch, we may find large clusters of Honey Mushrooms. They are highly ephemeral; common some years and rare in others. On nearby trees look up for the golden-brown Pholiotas, which may grow quite high on the trunks.

Don't give up when November blows in. Warm weather and wet ground may allow a few fleshy fungi to flourish for one last fling. But for consistent winter fungi watching, one must turn to the woody polypores known as brackets or shelves. Turkey Tail grows in colorful overlapping masses on deciduous trees. It persists all year but is easiest to see when the woods are bare. Paper Birches host several very distinctive polypores: the bulbous Birch Polypore and the Hoof Fungus or Tinder Polypore, which actually looks like a horse's hoof with the annual growth rings easily visible.

So don't give up on our northern fungi in late fall and winter. They are out there. Watch for them on your next autumn hike or even on a winter snowshoe trek!

Shaggy Mane

Meadow Mushroom

Honey Mushroom

Pholiota

Birch Polypore

Alcohol Inky

Puffballs

Giant Puffball

Turkey Tail

Hoof Fungus

GILLED *on* WOOD

Many of our gilled mushrooms that are found on wood grow in dense clusters. Few can forget the sight of a moss-covered log sprouting dozens of orange Fuzzy Foot mushrooms.

Not all grow on downed rotting logs. Look for Sharp-scaly Pholiota, Tree Volvariella and Netted Rhodotus on the trunks of living trees.

Some gilled fungi are less obvious in their attachment to wood. Jack O' Lantern, Platterfull Mushroom and Clustered Collybia often appear to be growing out of the ground but are usually rooted in subsurface decaying wood.

One of the finest forest edibles is a gilled-on-wood species; Oyster Mushrooms are a wonderful addition to a meal when sautéed in butter. But pick Oysters quickly as the fungus beetles will gladly make a meal of them before you!

Bleeding Fairy Helmet (Bleeding Mycena)

Mycena haematopus

Well-decayed birch and oak logs host colonies of this *Mycena*. The delicate mushrooms crowd together often in tufts with stem bases joined. Mature caps are helmet-like in shape. Their color varies from purple-gray to red-brown. Cap surface is faintly lined and a hump (umbo) is evident at the cap center. The cap's thin flesh, when moist, possesses something of a translucent quality. Cap edges are scalloped and often neatly upturned. The gills are whitish becoming spotted with red and brown. The narrow, hollow stem is colored like the cap.

A mass of coarse white hairs can be seen on its base. Occasionally you will find this mushroom covered by the fine, spiky threadings of the mold called *Spinellus fusiger* (see sidebar on next page).

The distinguishing feature of *Mycena haematopus* is its response to injury. Both cap and stem, when cut or broken, exude drops of blood-red latex, and hence, the common name, Bleeding Mycena.

Habitat
May be single, but usually in clusters on well-decayed wood of deciduous trees. Often on rotting birch. Saprophytic.

June	July	Aug.	Sept.

Cap: 3⅛–2"

Stem: 1–4"

Look for Bleeding Fairy Helmet singly or – more commonly – clustered on decaying wood

Spore Print

Gills: varied and adnate

Dog-Eat-Dog

In the volatile "dog-eat-dog" environment of the fungal world, you will frequently come across mushrooms enveloped in a cottony coat of mold, or "painted" white or some lurid color by the presence of another fungus. Such parasites can be very specific as to the choice of host mushroom. You may even be surprised to find some mushrooms living on other mushrooms, utilizing them as habitat and nourishment.

Here a Fairy Helmet (Mycena) is infected by Spinellus fusiger, a fungus related to bread molds. The dark bodies at the end of the hair-like stalks contain the parasite's spores. The parasite will allow the host to disperse its own spores — guaranteeing itself future hosts — but eventually reduce the Fairy Helmet to a puddly soup.

Pinwheel Marasmius *Marasmius rotula*

Clusters of these small, attractive mushrooms commonly occur on decaying deciduous wood. Each delicate cap is parasol-shaped with a broad central depression. The cap surface is dry, parchment-like. A neat arrangement of radiating pleats reach almost to the scalloped margin. White gills attach to the collar on a fine, wiry, shiny black stem. Sometimes a few brown, root-like hairs are attached to the stem base.

Resurrection!

Shriveled and inconspicuous, *Marasmius* species are rarely noticed during dry weather, but after rainy periods the tiny fungi flesh out, hence their nickname "resurrection fungi."

Habitat

Several to numerous on twigs and branches of dead or decaying wood. Common on beech.

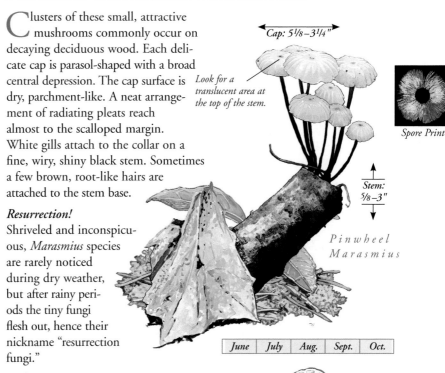

Cap: 5⅛–3¼"

Look for a translucent area at the top of the stem.

Spore Print

Stem: ⅝–3"

Pinwheel Marasmius

June	July	Aug.	Sept.	Oct.

Gills: Adnate and attached at collar

Fuzzy Foot *Xeromphalina campanella*

Also known as Golden Trumpets, this fungus produces a veritable army of small fruiting bodies exclusively on conifer wood and conifer debris.

A tough, slender, curved stem supports the cap. It is yellow near the top and dark red-brown below with a dense tufting of long, bright tawny hairs at its base that earns it the name, "Fuzzy Foot." The individual mushroom cap is rounded to flat with a pit-like central depression. Cap surface

Look for cross-veins: small, intersecting ridges between the gills.

is moist, but not slimy, and colored yellow, orange or tawny brown with darker tones on the disk (cap center). Cap has thin and pliant flesh and a prominently-lined and turned-down margin. Narrow gills are set far apart and extend down the stem. They are yellow to dull orange and have cross-veins (see inset illustration).

Spore Print

Habitat

Large clusters on decaying moss-covered logs, stumps and woody debris of conifers—Hemlock, Eastern White Pine or Jack Pine. Saprophytic.

Cap: 1/8– 1 3/8"

Fuzzy Foot is so specialized in its choice of host that a fruiting confirms that the stump or log is surely a conifer.

Gills: decurrent and widely spaced

These fungi have fuzzy feet! Look for the dense tuft of hairs at the base of the stalk.

Stem: 5/8–3"

Fuzzy Foot

June	July	Aug.	Sept.	Oct.	Nov.

An Eerie Green Light in the Night

A fascinating feature of the next fungus, Omphalotus olearius, is its glow-in-the-dark capability. Like a number of fungi, the fruiting body and mycelium emit an eerie greenish glow, observable in moonless woods or in a totally darkened room. The glow lasts 40 to 50 hours after the specimen is collected and may be bright enough to see each individual gill. If it doesn't glow, wrap it in wax paper, place indoors and try again in two to three hours.

Tales are told of folks placing pieces of wood bearing glowing mycelium to mark a path for night travel. Some claim to have read by the light. It can be imagined that through the ages humans have been startled and perplexed, perhaps terrified, when they encountered the glowing fungus.

How does a mushroom present this display of light? Scientists theorize that it is caused by a process called bioluminescence. "Photo proteins,"—units combining specific chemicals and oxygen—are triggered to produce light by addition of calcium or other ions to the system. The light in these mushrooms is produced by a chemical reaction and is not a glow achieved by absorbing light from outside sources.

Jack O' Lantern *Omphalotus olearius (Omphalotus illudens)*

This fungus produces huge clumps of sturdy, brilliant-orange mushrooms at the base of stumps and on the roots of living trees. It also fruits on buried wood. Mature caps are large, flat and depressed with a low pointed central knob. They are usually orange, but sometimes are a ruddy-brown color. The surface of the cap is smooth and streaked with dark fibrils. The margin is incurved, wavy and splits with age. Cap flesh is thin, firm and pale yellow. There are narrow, sharp-edged gills tightly packed under the cap. The individual gill is bow-shaped, narrowing at each end.

Gills run down the stalk for some distance. The tough, fibrous stalk is dry, smooth and colored like the cap. With age the stalk surface may become downy or scaly.

Evil Jack

This poisonous species should not be mistaken for the eminently edible Chanterelle. Its sharp-edged gills, growth on decaying wood or living trees and strong disagreeable odor give it away. *Omphalotus olearius* is not only dangerous to humans but is a powerful pathogen of trees, eventually killing its host tree.

Habitat

Dense clusters on buried wood, roots and stumps of oaks and other deciduous wood. Often grows where trees have been removed. Sometimes seems to be growing from the ground. May be a parasite on broadleaf trees. Saprophytic or parasitic.

Jack O' Lantern

Cap: 2-6"

Stem: 2–8"

Called Jack O' Lantern because it may glow in the dark. But, the light emitted is greenish, not orange (see sidebar on previous page).

Inexperienced mushroomers may mistake this species for Chanterelle. But note the sharp-edged gills, dense clustered growth on wood —characteristics not shared with the Chanterelles.

Gills: decurrent and crowded

Spore Print

| July | Aug. | Sept. | Oct. |

Sharp-scaly Pholiota *Pholiota squarrosoides*

Mounds of spiky, yellowish caps on scaly stems cling to living trees or hardwood stumps; clumps of 50 or more are not unheard of. The cap of the mushroom is rounded, with a low umbo. A gelatinous, sticky surface underlies stands of sharp, erect scales (veil remnants) that are scattered near the margin, but concentrated over the cap center. The brownish-orange scales are dry and have recurved tips. Older caps, which are weather-washed, may lose the scales. The white gills are crowded and attached, usually with a notch near the stem. As the spores mature, the gills become rusty-brown. There is a sturdy, yellowish stem, circled near the top by a pale, cottony ring that may disappear due to the wear-and-tear of the elements. The stem top is whitish and silky. Below the ring it is covered with coarse down-curved brown-orange scales.

Habitat

Clusters are found on living or dead deciduous wood—trees, stumps and logs of birch, alder, beech and maple. Occasionally on decaying conifers. Saprophytic or parasitic.

Cap: 1-4"

Stem: 2–6"

In wet weather or in old age, the cap has a gelatinous, sticky surface with scattered dry scales.

Sharp-scaly Pholiota

Aug.	Sept.	Oct.

Gills: attached, notched and crowded

Spore Print

Scaly Pholiota

Pholiota squarrosa

"Scaly" nicely sums up the character of this mushroom. Its cap and stem are both closely covered with upright scales giving it a shaggy charm. The basic cap is pinkish-tan to straw-colored, sometimes with a greenish-yellow margin. The cap is bluntly rounded when young, becoming bell-shaped in age. The scales, formed by the break-up of the cap cuticle, cover the entire surface and are persistent. The margin adds to the mushroom's shaggy appearance with its fringe of veil material. Gills are attached, close and narrow. As the

Spore Print

Cap: 1-4"

Stem: 2–3"

Scaly Pholiota

mushroom ages, gills take on a greenish tint and finally become rusty-brown. The stalk is thick, tapering down to an enlarged base. A fragile, yellowish ring (or zone of shredded veiling) is found on the upper stem. The stem is smooth and solid above the ring. Below, countless down-turned scales, like those on the cap, cover the surface.

Habitat

Pholiota squarrosa fruits in tufts or clusters on the trunks, stumps and roots of hardwoods and conifers.

July	Aug.	Sept.	Oct.

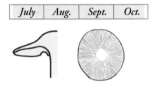

*Gills:
attached, notched and crowded*

Split Gill *Schizophyllum commune*

Split Gill may be the most widely distributed mushroom in the world. It is found on every continent except at the North and South Poles. The small, gray to white, fan-shaped caps grow in groups or lines on dead branches and logs of hardwoods. The caps have a conspicuous covering of white hairs. Caps are tough and leathery with a scalloped, inrolled margin. Stemless, the caps attach directly to the wood. Gills radiate

← Cap: 3/8 – 1 5/8"

May be the most widespread mushroom in the world.

*Split
Gill*

from the mushroom's point of attachment and curve outward to the margin. Gills are deeply grooved or split lengthwise (see inset illustration above). These curves and lines give the tiny fungus an attractive, arty touch. To survive dry times, the mushroom cap curls down over the gills. Once wetter days return, caps quickly revive.

Note the very distinctive doubled rows: the "Split gills" are really two adjacent but separate gills.

Habitat

Solitary, scattered or in overlapping clusters on dead branches, logs or stumps of hardwood trees. May also appear on straw bales and driftwood or boards of hickory, walnut, elm or oak. Has even been found growing on animal matter: whalebones and the scar tissue of a human mouth! Saprophytic.

June	July	Aug.	Sept.	Oct.	Nov.

Fruiting June - November; Can be seen year round.

Crinkle Gill *Plicaturopsis crispa*

An interesting little fungus that is found on dead hardwood in overlapping clusters. Caps are fan-shaped with deeply lobed or wavy margins. Mature caps have zoning of tan-brown and red-brown with cream-colored margins. The fertile underside has shallow, gill-like folds that are notably crimped (wavy). A close look will show that they are forked and are joined by numerous cross veins. Caps curl when dry. They revive and become soft and flexible in wet conditions.

Undersides: not really gills! Look for shallow, gill-like folds.

Habitat

Overlapping clusters on branches and trunks of hardwoods: beech, birch, cherry. Most often seen during or after rainy periods.

◄— *Cap: 3/8–7/8"* —►

Year-round

Crinkle Gill

Oyster Mushroom *Pleurotus ostreatus*

This mushroom possesses a special beauty. It flares out from the host wood singly, shelf-like, or in tight, overlapping clusters, displaying a smooth clean cap, an arching inrolled margin and a wide sweeping curve of gills. It fruits on stumps, aspen and willow snags and other decaying woods (but not usually on conifer).

CHOICE

Often abundant at the time when folks are busy scouting the woods for morels.

The cap is shell-shaped or fan-like and may be cream, gray or brown. The surface is moist, but not slimy, and cap flesh is thick creamy-white, firm but tender. The cap is often attached directly to the wood (sessile), but a short, sturdy, curving stem may be found. It holds the cap laterally or centrally depending on where the fruiting body is positioned on the host wood. The stem has a velvety, hair-covered base. The radiating white gills have moderately wide spacing and extend down to the point of attachment. Many shorter gills are interspersed with the full length gills.

Two forms may be observed. The light-capped ones grow in warmer weather, the dark-capped ones appear in cooler times.

◄— *Cap: 2-8"*

Stem: if present, up to 1 1/2" tall

When growing out of the side of a log, the stem is lateral or absent, but centralized when above the log.

Oyster Mushroom

Note the gills' wide spacing, the many interspersed shorter gills and the cross-veins.

Habitat

Large clusters, often overlapping, on stumps, logs and trunks of deciduous trees, especially visible on standing dead aspens. Has been reported on elm, cottonwood, alder, oak, willow, poplar, beech, aspen and maple. Saprophytic and parasitic.

Edible Complex

This easy-to-recognize mushroom is actually part of a complex of very similar mushrooms that are hard to separate and identify, even by microscopic features. However, they are all choice edibles. Once established in a patch of woods, the Oyster makes itself at home and can be found fruiting annually.

Best to gather this mushroom quickly when you spot it, as it soon will have a compliment of shiny black fungus beetles who will ruin the caps by tunneling through them.

Look who's coming for dinner: Oyster Mushrooms are often home to prolific tiny pleasing fungus beetles (Family Erotylidae) such as Triplax thoracica.

Oil Eater

Oyster Mushroom spores are used in straw mats to help collect and eat oil spills. Acids and enzymes released by their mycelium breaks down the complex molecular structure of petroleum-based contaminants. They were used recently off the coast of Spain.

Spore Print

May	June	July	Aug.	Sept.	Oct.

Attack of the Killer Hyphae!

The hyphae of Oyster Mushrooms produce tiny appendages called stephanocysts which secrete a potent toxin. Nematodes (small, microscopic roundworms) which are unfortunate enough to cross paths with the stephanocysts are quickly paralyzed. Other specialized hyphae then find and penetrate the nematode's outer layer and digest its inner contents. This, of course, spells the end for the nematode but makes a tasty nitrogen snack for the fungus.

And not only nematodes need beware; scientists have also observed bacteria colonies being attacked. Once P. ostreatus detects a nearby colony, it sends out a very fine hyphae that penetrates the bacterial colony and forms specialized feeding cells inside. These break down and consume the bacteria, transferring the nutrients back to the main mycelial body.

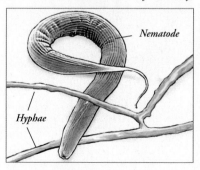

Nematode

Hyphae

Netted Rhodotus *Rhodotus palmatus*

A very special find whose range seems to be limited to Northeast North America. The rounded apricot-pink to reddish cap is ornamented with a unique network of ridges and shallow pits. The flesh of the cap has a rubbery feel and appears gelatin-like. The pale pink gills are broad, connected by veins and are also rather rubbery. They appear whitish when young, becoming pink to salmon from spores.

Cap: 1-2"

When clustered, the overlapping caps often adhere to each other because of the gummy cap surfaces.

The pink stem completes the con-colored array. It is tough and fibrous, off-center and typically bent. The mushroom is said to have a pleasant odor.

Fruitings do not happen every year and never occur more than once on the same wood.

Stem: 1-2"

Habitat
Solitary to scattered on old dead hardwood logs, trunks or posts. Especially found on maple, sometimes elm and poplar.

Fungal Non-Conformist
This mushroom's unusual combination of features, color, netted cap surface, gelatinous flesh and its spore color, set it apart from the traditional categories, so mycologists created a new genus, *Rhodotus*, to accommodate it. *Rhodotus palmatus* is the lone species in the genus.

June	July	Aug.	Sept.

Spore Print

Gills: decurrent

Netted Rhodotus

What's in a Name?

A mushroom's species name often focuses on a notable part of its make-up. It could be the shape of stem, special coloration, shape and character of the cap, a particular habit of growth or a specialized habitat. In the case of R. palmatus, the given name points to the likeness between the mushroom's cap with its pattern of ridges and the shape and lined surface of the human palm.

Tree Volvariella *Volvariella bombycina*

Some mushrooms are simply lovely to behold; this is one of them. It has a wide, white, silky cap, broad, well-spaced gills which are pink at maturity, and a shiny, curved stem. The soft fragile cap is oval initially and then becomes dome-shaped. A coating of fine white hairs gives the surface a silken sheen and hairs form a fringe on the cap margin. The broad gills are crowded and not attached to the stem. They are veined and their edges often eroded. Many shorter gills (lamellae) mingle with those of regular length. As the spores begin to be dispersed, the gills take on a pale pink coloration. The stem is firm and smooth, usually curved and enlarged at the base. The stem base is encased in a deep, loose sack-like volva which is thick-walled, white to brownish and often pocked or scaly.

Can be distinguished from members of the dangerous *Amanita* family by its growth on wood, very deep sack-like volva and hairy, silken cap. This easy-to-identify, hard-to-find species causes heartwood rot in some trees. It may have an odor of radishes.

Cap: 2–8"

Stem: 2³⁄₈–8"

Look for a base encased in a thick, white, yellowish or brownish, sack-like volva.

Tree Volvariella

The Tree Volvariella starts its life in a pronounced sack-like volva as seen in this cross-section.

Culinary Cultivation

In 19ᵗʰ century Italy this species was cultivated as a desirable edible. Today, mushrooms of the genus *Volvariella* account for 16 percent of total production of cultivated mushrooms in the world.

Habitat

Found on dead, decaying wood and in wounds of living trees, sometimes a considerable height off the ground—maple, beech, oak, elm and box elder. Has also been found on stored wood and buildings. Saprophytic.

Gills: spaced and free

Spore Print

| July | Aug. | Sept. | Oct. |

Deer Mushroom *Pluteus cervinus*

Walk a stretch of forest land where there are large quantities of downed, rotting birch logs, and chances are you will find this mushroom. It usually has an erect stance among decaying wood and white curls of birchbark.

In form, the fruiting body resembles a long-handled umbrella, partially open. The cap is dark brown to smoky gray with a low central hump (umbo) and is lined radially with imbedded darker fibers. The cap is moist, but not slimy. Broad, white gills are free and crowded under the cap and soon become pinkish due to the release of mature spores. Gills are rounded in back. The long white stem is smooth and firm.

Cap: 1–4¾"

Stem: 4–8"

Crush the stem to note an odor of radishes.

May	June	July	Aug.	Sept.	Oct.

"Free" gills are not attached to stem

Gills

Stem

Free Gills

This is a good species for observing what mycologists call free gills. Hold a specimen, stem up, in your palm. Look down to where the stem and cap join. You can see that there is a gap around the stem and that the gills stop before reaching the stem.

Habitat

In addition to birch, *P. cervinus* can be found fruiting on broad-leafed and conifer timber.

Spore Print

Clustered Collybia

Acervata means "clustered," and these little mushrooms live up to their name. When fresh and moist, the caps are a dark red-brown with paler margins. When dry or aged, they become pale tan. Caps are rounded to almost flat and very smooth. After rains they may look water-soaked, but they are not slimy. The narrow gills are whitish-pink and the smooth, hollow and flexible stalk is a dark wine-brown with fine white hairs

Cap: 1-2"

July	Aug.	Sept.	Oct.

Collybia acervata

covering the lower half. Stem bases are joined and seem bound together by a thick mass of mycelium.

Habitat
Large compact groups can be found on rotting conifer stumps, logs and buried conifer wood. Sometimes appears to be growing from the soil.

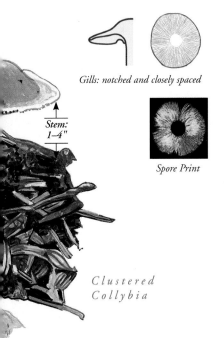

Gills: notched and closely spaced

Stem:
1–4"

Spore Print

*Clustered
Collybia*

Platterfull Mushroom *Megacollybia (Tricholomopsis) platyphylla*

This mushroom is one of the earliest gilled mushrooms to appear in spring. It fruits on rotting logs, wood debris and buried wood in groups and in tufts with joined stem bases. The cap of mature specimens is silver-gray to gray-brown with smooth surface streaked radially by darker fibrils. The cap is relatively flat with sunken center and small umbo and its margin is thin, wavy and often split with age. The flesh of the cap is pliant and fragile.

The very broad, ragged-edged, white gills are adnate to notched, with conspicuous cross veining. There is no veil; the stalk is smooth, sturdy and becomes hollow with age. A scattering of flattened white hairs and grayish coloration can often be seen at the base.

The fascinating feature of this mushroom is the white, shoestring-like rhizomorphs attached to the stalk base which are root-like and spread widely and deeply into the substrate.

Spore Print

Habitat
Single to scattered on well-decayed logs, stumps, wood debris or buried wood in hardwood or conifer woods. May even fruit on leaf litter. Saprophytic.

Caps are impressive in size, sometimes as big as a salad plate.

← Cap: 2–5" →

Gills: varied length, spaced and free or nearly so

Stem:
3–5"

*Platterfull
Mushroom*

| May | June | July | Aug. | Sept. | Oct. |

Dig to find white mycelial cords (rhizomorphs) attached to the base.

Honey Mushroom *Armillaria mellea*

They are called Honeys, Cinnamon Tops, Buttons, Stumpies and a myriad of other names. The mushrooms produced by the fungus, *Armillaria mellea* are sought after, gathered and eaten by thousands of folks. Probably in a mushroom popularity contest they would take top prize, at least for their quantity. The mushrooms are found in massive colonies on the stumps, buried wood and on trunks of living hardwoods, especially Northern Red Oak. Caps come in a variety of colors; honey-yellow, tan, pink-brown to red-brown. The cap's surface is covered by a scattering of brown-black, sharp, tufted hairs, with a concentration of them over the cap's central knob. These scale-like tufts are a hallmark of the Honey Mushroom. The cap is slimy when wet. Flesh is thick and white. On older caps the margin may be wavy or flaring. Often, in a dense cluster of the mushrooms, you will find lower caps covered with the dusty powder of spores released from caps above.

Gills are well-separated, white to pale yellow. They are attached to the stem and somewhat decurrent. In older mushrooms the gills may be stained yellow to rust. The stalk is pith-filled and later hollow. It is thick, tough and fibrous, often with a bulbous base. The white membranous ring, or remnants of it, should be found on the upper stalk.

Mycelium from these mushrooms may cause the aborted phase of *Entoloma* (page 124).

Habitat

Grows in clusters at base of trees, near stumps; living or dead. Besides Northern Red Oak, it grows on birch,

Cap: 1-4"

Honey Mushroom

| Aug. | Sept. | Oct. |

Stem: 2–6"

Instead of generating food from sunlight, Indian Pipe (Monotropa uniflora) — which is a flowering plant, not a fungus — parasitizes the Honey Mushroom that, in turn, takes nutrients from oaks and other trees.

Gills: adnate to slightly decurrent and well-separated

Spore Print

poplar, maple and beech. Saprophytic or Parasitic.

A Honey of an Edible?

Though many eat this mushroom, there needs to be caution in identifying and cooking. There are a number of toxic look-alikes! Also, this mushroom needs thorough cooking, and even then, some people experience stomach upsets.

Deadly Shoestrings

Honey Mushrooms are listed as one of the top ten pathogens of trees, especially hardwoods. The fungus produces a root rot called "shoestring rot." Under proper conditions the mushroom spores infect woody shrubs, bases of dead trees or stumps. These serve as a food base from which rhizomorphs are produced. Rhizomorphs are black or red-brown shoestring-like cords of hyphae, about the diameter of a pencil. They can grow through the soil for many feet and when they come into contact with the roots of a susceptible host, they penetrate the bark, moving directly into the cambium and bark tissues. White fans of mycelium develop under the bark. (Both the rhizomorphs and fans can be seen by peeling away the bark of dead tree.) Decay occurs in the woody tissue of roots and base of the infected tree or shrub. Sometimes the process is undetected until the mushroom fruits and its crowd of mushroom caps is seen. Chiefly threatened by this fungus are Northern Red Oak, maples, birches, apples and conifers.

Young Honey Mushroom buttons

Glow-in-the-Dark Fungus

Under certain conditions (especially following a good rain), mycelium of *Armillaria mellea* may be luminescent in host wood. It glows in the dark creating an eerie light called "foxfire" on the forest floor.

World's Largest Living Thing

"**S**tep up ladies and gentleman! Beneath your feet is the world's largest living thing!" It's true. A close relative of the Honey Mushroom is reputed to be one of the largest living things ever discovered. In Michigan's Upper Peninsula near Crystal Falls, researchers, using DNA testing and other genetic data, found the interconnected rhizomorphs of a single Armillaria galica spread through, and underlying some 30 acres of forest. The fungus is estimated to be 1,500 years old.

In the state of Washington, a growth of another immense Armillaria (A. ostoyae) has been discovered, covering about 2.5 square miles of land. A still larger Armillaria ostoyae has been discovered and studied in Oregon. Its fungal outline stretches 3.5 miles across and it extends an average of three feet into the ground. It is estimated to have existed over 2,000 years.

MINN.

MICHIGAN

WISCONSIN

Velvet-footed Pax *Paxillus atrotomentosus*

A group of these mushrooms is an impressive sight. They emerge sometimes four or five at a time from well-rotted conifer wood. They are large and sturdy. The dry, downy cap of this mushroom varies from yellow to rust-brown and becomes darker with age, displaying a matting of brown-black wool. It is flat at maturity with an in-rolled margin. The flesh of the cap is tough, thick and watery and yellowish-buff in color. Sometimes when the cap is cut, you find a pinkish spotting or marbling in the flesh. The entire top skin, called the cuticle, can easily be pulled away from the cap. The dull yellow gills reach a short way down the stalk. They fork near the stalk and sometimes form

Cap: 1 1/2–6"

Stem: 3 1/2–5"

Velvet-footed Pax

pore-like structures. The gills easily detach from the lower cap surface.

Most striking is the appearance of the solid, bulky stalk. It is light yellow at the top but most of its surface is covered with a velvety mat of brown-black hairs. The stalk often has an off-center or lateral attachment to the cap.

Habitat

Alone, scattered or in clusters on well-decayed conifer logs, stumps or buried wood; especially pine. Saprophytic.

A Case of Rot

Paxillus atrotomentosus is one of the mushrooms that causes brown rot. If you lift the mushroom from its host base, you will notice that the wood left behind is crumbly, brown and often broken

into cube-like pieces. Fungi that cause brown rot are able to digest only the cellulose component of the wood. When the cellulose is destroyed, what remains is the brown lignum.

Dyer's Note

Dye extracted from this fungus can turn yarns a lovely moss-green.

July	Aug.	Sept.	Oct.

Spore Print

Gills: varied length and decurrent. Can form pore-like structures

Velvet Foot *Flammulina velutipes*

Tufts of these petite mushrooms with orange caps appear on hardwood stumps. The orange-yellow to burnt-orange cap is smooth, shiny and sticky with a dark center and light margin. The margin is inrolled and faintly lined. Cap flesh is pale yellow. Gills are attached, cream-colored, narrow and close. Long and short gills intermix and gill edges are minutely fringed with fibers. The feature to especially note is the tough, tapering stem made dark and velvety by brown-black hairs. The stem is hollow and may be curved or twisted. The base often has a coating of white mycelium. This is one of the only mushrooms fruiting above ground during the winter. Winter fruiting can be expected if there is sufficient moisture and several consecutive days with temperatures above freezing.

Habitat
Found on hardwood stumps, logs, roots, and sometimes on living trees

Enotake (Enokitake)
A cultivated form of this mushroom called Enotake is sold in Asian specialty stores and in supermarkets. It has long, spaghetti-like stems and tiny caps with little resemblance to the wild Velvet Foot. The mushrooms are packaged in bunches and sold as an unusual addition to salads. They are said to taste like grapes.

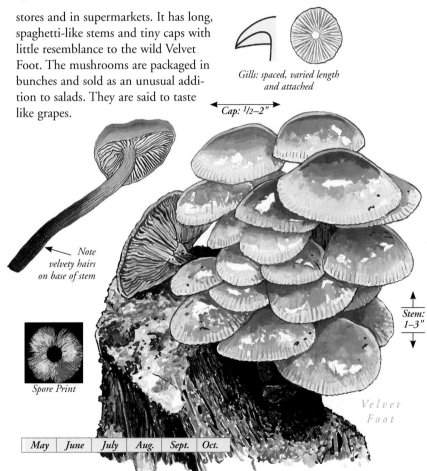

Gills: spaced, varied length and attached

Cap: 1/2–2"

Note velvety hairs on base of stem

Spore Print

Stem: 1–3"

Velvet Foot

| May | June | July | Aug. | Sept. | Oct. |

Deadly Galerina *Galerina autumnalis*

Looks can deceive. This small brown mushroom appears innocent and harmless, but it contains a deadly toxin.

The thin, smooth cap is dark brown to tawny brown, flat at maturity and may have a low central hump. Cap margin is finely lined, and its outer edges quickly fade to orange-yellow. In moist conditions it is somewhat tacky. The close, brownish gills are broadly attached and may extend a short way down the stem. As spores are released, the gills take on a rusty color.

The narrow, hollow stem is dark-brown and coated with fine grayish-white hairs. A fibrous ring circles the upper stem, but this may gradually wear away. The stem base, often enlarged, has a matting of white mycelium.

Deadly Toxin

Amanitin is the toxin that makes Deadly Galerina deadly. It destroys liver and kidney function. Since this mushroom often grows on the same wood where edibles fruit, it is important to know how to distinguish Deadly Galerina.

Habitat

Scattered or clustered on decaying hardwoods or conifers. Saprophytic.

Deadly Galerina

The cap is radially lined when moist.

Cap: 1/2–2 1/2

Stem: 1–3"

Note a ring or membraneous zone.

Sept.	Oct.	Nov.

Sometimes May and June

Spore Print

Brick Top

Colonies of these red-capped mushrooms push up at the base of hardwood stumps and from crevices in logs. The groupings are often so tightly packed that stems of the individual mushrooms become twisted and compressed as they grow to maturity. The smooth dry caps are brick-red, darker at the center and typically with pallid, pinkish-yellow margins. Younger caps are rounded. Caps of mature specimens are flat sometimes with a low central knob. Cap edges are down-turned and may be downy with fragments of veil tissue. The pale yellow cap flesh is thick and firm.

Gills are narrow, close and attached to the stem. They are pale purple-gray initially, but quickly become blackish. The upper stem has a yellow zone where veil remnants form a fragile ring. The lower portion of the stem gradually becomes dull-brown to gray in color and, at times, is shaggy with a covering of fine, red-brown fibers. The stem hollows with age. It stains yellow where cut or bruised.

Also called *Hypholoma sublateritium*.

Naematoloma sublateritium

Habitat
On hardwood stumps and logs.
Saprophytic.

A Brick Top doesn't have a brick bottom—the gill color in mature specimens is dark purple-gray or purple-brown.

Stem: 2–4"

Cap: 1 – 4"

Brick Top

Spore Print

Aug. | Sept. | Oct.

Plums & Custard (Variegated Mop)

Tricholomopsis rutilans

Plums and Custard

Spore Print

The quaint common name, "Plums and Custard," is based on cap color—the underlying surface is creamy custard-yellow and the overlay of scale-like fibers is a deep plum-red. This coloration is particularly striking in young specimens.

The velvet-like, reddish scaling is concentrated at the cap center. The cap is bell-shaped, becoming flatter at maturity. There is a low umbo. Flesh of the cap is thick and firm. A yellow staining may be noted.

Narrow, sulfur-yellow gills are notched where they join the stem. Numerous tiers of shorter gills are inter-mixed with regular gills. Gill edges are frayed and irregularly torn.

The thick, leathery stem has a slight enlargement at the base and becomes hollow with age. The surface, particularly the lower portion, is finely coated with fibrous scales colored like those on the cap.

Cap: 1 1/2–4"

Stem: 2–4"

Habitat
Decaying conifer wood and roots.
Saprophytic.

Aug. | Sept. | Oct.

Spore Print

Night Light *Panellus stipticus*

Night Light gills by day

Finding colonies of this small shelf fungus can lead to a fun experiment. Place in a lidded jar with a touch of water. Now bring to a pitch black closet; the mushrooms will emit a steady greenish glow. This glow can be maintained for a week or more!

Most caps are grouped in multiple tiers with much overlapping. They are fan-shaped, thin, leathery and depressed at the point where they join the stem. The upper surface is densely hairy and is zoned concentrically in pale shades of brown. Cap margins becomes flared and tattered with age. The salmon-colored gills lining the underside of the cap are narrow and crowded. They are markedly straight and joined by numerous cross-veins.

Stem: 1/8–1/2"

Cap: 3/8–1 1/2"

May–Dec

Night Light

Always grows on log or stumps, never on living trees.

There is a short white stem that narrows abruptly to its base. Note that, where it attaches to the side of the cap, the stem is compressed into a small, flat semi-circle. The stem base is covered with tufts of hairs.

As its scientific name implies, this mushroom has styptic (blood-stopping) chemical compounds.

Habitat
On decaying hardwood logs. Saprophytic.

The gills of fresh specimens produce a green glow at night.

Train Wrecker *Neolentinus lepideus (Lentinus lepideus)*

This large mushroom is characterized by a stiff, firm cap and stem, and its habit of sprouting from railroad ties, telephone poles, fence posts, decking and even boring old logs and stumps.

The buff cap is rounded at first, but flat at maturity. Cap margin is incurved.

N. lepideus is capable of invading and fruiting on some treated woods. In the past it attacked railroad ties causing derailments, and so, earned its common name, Train Wrecker.

Drops of moisture rest on the margin of young caps. The cap surface is very distinct with its somewhat circular pattern of coarse reddish-brown scales. These large scales occur in patches and are tightly pressed against the surface. Cracks can be found in caps of older specimens. Cap flesh is white.

The broad, white to buff gills vary from close to sub-distant. A notch can be observed on the gills where they attach to the stem. Gills are often

Cap: 2–10"

The gills have serrated or jagged edges.

Stem: 1–6"

decurrent and create lines at the apex of the stem. As the mushroom matures, the gills develop serrated edges.

The tough, solid stem is colored like the cap and narrows abruptly to a pointed base. It may be slightly off-center. A pallid, membranous ring hangs at the top of the stem but becomes weathered and eventually wears away. A crowd of scruffy, brownish recurved scales cover the stem below the ring.

Cap, stem and gills of this mushroom stain yellowish to rusty brown when handled. The mushroom has the pleasant odor of licorice

Habitat
Singly or in groups on conifer logs and stumps, occasionally oak. Also found on construction timber, fence posts and train tracks. Saprophytic.

Spore Print

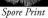

| May | June | July | Aug. | Sept. |

Gills: adnate (left) to slightly decurrent (right)

GILLED *on* OTHER

Not all gilled fungi sprout from the ground or decaying wood; some sprout from cones, leaves or even other mushrooms. *Baeospora myosura* requires the cones of conifers as a substrate. It is often found on fallen Eastern White Pine cones. *Marasmius capillaris* needs fallen oak leaves; it sprouts from the leaf veins. A unique little parasite is the Powder Cap; clusters of cute little white mushrooms stand triumphantly from the tops of defeated rotting masses of old *Lactarius* and *Russula* caps.

Even "Moose marbles" are an acceptable substrate for some gilled fungi; Dung Roundhead fruits from the droppings of Moose, deer, cows and horses. Keep an eye out for this fascinating fungus…and watch out for the dung too!

Powder Cap *Asterophora lycoperdoides (Nyctalis asterophora)*

Clusters of these tiny parasitic mushrooms can be found on old *Russulas* and *Lactarius* caps. They resemble a puffball when young; but this parasite has gills. The entire fruiting body starts white, eventually becoming misshapen and densely covered with brown powder. This fascinating fungus parasitizes other mushrooms, often after the host mushroom has been reduced to a blackish, unidentifiable mush. We do know that they often parasitize species in the *Russula nigricans* group.

Habitat
Clustered on other decaying mushrooms, especially *Lactarius* and *Russula*. May be hard to recognize the host mushroom. Parasitic.

Puffballs? Not!
These small mushrooms may be mistaken for puffballs due to their poorly formed gills and rounded cap, but there are no parasitic puffballs.

The white Powder Caps will eventually be covered in a fine brown powder (hence its common name).

Cap: 3/8–3/4"

The host mushroom is often not this well preserved; it may be just an unrecognizable black mass of mush.

Spore Print

| July | Aug. | Sept. | Oct. | Nov. |

Oak-leaf Marasmius *Marasmius capillaris*

A fun find; this delicate mushroom grows on fallen leaves of broadleaf trees, especially oak, during periods of prolonged rain. Each individual emerges from a leaf vein. They sport a deeply grooved umbrella-shaped cap with a tiny central depression.

Spore Print

The cap is buff-colored and has a parchment-like texture. The white gills are set far apart. The black, shiny stem is almost as fine as a hair and is wiry and tough. The mushroom appears quickly after rain and disappears quickly as the woods dry out.

Habitat
Deciduous woods. Scattered to gregarious on dead oak leaves. Saprophytic.

Gills: widely spaced, varied length and attached

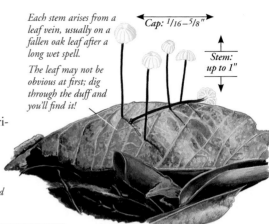

Each stem arises from a leaf vein, usually on a fallen oak leaf after a long wet spell.

The leaf may not be obvious at first; dig through the duff and you'll find it!

Cap: 1/16–5/8"

Stem: up to 1"

Oak-leaf Marasmius

Conifer-cone Baeospora *Baeospora myosura*

Conifer-cone Baeospora

Cap: up to 3/4"

Stem: 5/8–2"

Look for fruitings on white pine cones after days of rain.

Sept. | Oct.

*B*aeospora *myosura* inhabits the small world of a single pinecone; often the cone of an Eastern White Pine. The mushroom has a thin, delicate dome-shaped cap with a sunken center, smooth moist surface and an inrolled, wavy margin. Cap color is cinnamon or brownish mauve. The narrow white gills are attached and exceptionally crowded. The hollow, spindly stem is initially white but becomes brownish. Its dry surface is covered by minute white hairs and it's often vertically grooved.

Long, loose hairs are found on the stem base. The mushroom is attached to the cone by short white filaments. Optimal fruiting time is during prolonged wet periods in fall.

Spore Print

Gills: crowded, varied length and attached

Coprophiles

Grazing herbivores swallow thousands of spores, some of which will have their prayers answered: such spores have a special coating that makes them impervious to gut enzymes that eagerly digest other spores. Once the dung is voided, these spores germinate, grow and fruit. The fruiting bodies produce more spores, and with luck, some will be eaten, whereupon the whole process will begin again.

It's fun to culture dung fungi. Just get a few pellets of deer or sheep dung and place them in a yogurt container on a moistened paper towel. A few days later, you'll see dozens of Dung Cannons (Pilobolus sp.) speckling the dish's lid with their violently discharged black spores. Still later, you might see Inky Caps rising up from their chosen pellets, and with luck you might eventually see some tiny yellow cup fungi (Lasiobolus or Trichobolus sp.) on the pellets. So what are you waiting for?

— Lawrence Millman
author of *Fascinating Fungi of New England*

Dung Roundhead *Stropharia semiglobata*

The shiny, yellow-brown cap of this small dung dweller is usually well rounded (shaped like a half-globe) with a thin, pale, down-turned margin. The cap surface is smooth, hairless and noticeably slimy when wet. It has attached, grayish gills that are very broad with minutely hairy edges. In young specimens they're gray but soon become purple-black as the dark spores are released. The stem is slender, but it's tough, straight and relatively long. A fragile tissue-like ring may be found on the upper stalk, darkened by falling spores. Sometimes there is little more than a dark fibrous ring zone. Below the ring area, the stalk is exceedingly slimy.

There are a number of other small mushrooms that, like Dung Roundhead, enjoy the comfort and amenities of horse and cow dung. Some are hallucinogenic, some toxic.

Habitat
Paths, fields and anywhere dung-producing animals produce dung!

Gills:
adnate and closely spaced

Spore Print

◄— Cap: 3/8–2" —►

Look for the thin ring that is normally dusted dark from the falling spores.

Stem: 4–6"

D u n g   R o u n d h e a d

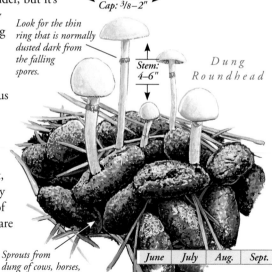

Sprouts from dung of cows, horses, deer and moose.

| June | July | Aug. | Sept. |

Yellow Parasol *Lepiota lutea (Leucocoprinus birnbaumii)*

What a fun surprise to find a troop of these bright, parasol-shaped mushrooms emerging from the soil of one of your potted plants. Their thin, delicate caps vary from pale to brilliant yellow sometimes with a hint of green.

The caps are dry with a powdery or finely scaly surface. In mature specimens, the caps bear deep grooves that radiate from the knobby center out to the margin. The gills and stem are yellow. Gills are free, closely set and hairy-edged. The stem is slender but usually enlarged at its base. Stem surface may be smooth or powdery. A small, moveable, collar-like ring circles the top of the stem.

Spore Print

Habitat
In addition to the potted plants in your home or green house, these mushrooms can also emerge from compost and woody debris outside. Saprophytic.

July	Aug.	Sept.	Oct.

Year-round indoors

Yellow Parasol

Cap: 1–2 ¹/₂"

Stem: 1–3"

Commonly found in flowerpots

Gills: adnate and free

NON-GILLED *on* GROUND

Don't be fooled by the Boletes. *Boletus*, *Suillus* and *Leccinum* mushrooms look like ordinary run-of-the-mill gilled fungi, but a peek beneath the cap will reveal that they lack gills and have about a million holes (pores). These are the tubes from which the spores are released. The unique Hedgehog Mushroom has "teeth" below the cap on which the spores reside.

Morels are also included in this group. In the North Woods, the Black Morel is the most common.

Many other strange fungi are found in this category: the cups, corals, jellies, puffballs and the bizarre Dog Stinkhorn.

Note that some species (several puffballs and bird's-nest species) can be found on both the ground and on very rotted wood.

King Bolete *Boletus edulis*

A large, handsome and bulbous mushroom. Its thick cap is broadly rounded to nearly plane with an even margin. The surface is smooth, sometimes slightly wrinkled and feels sticky when wet. Cap color varies widely from yellow-brown, red-brown, tan, dark red to cinnamon buff. The flesh is firm and white. The pore surface starts white, becomes yellowish and, with the release of the spores, turns to olive-yellow. The stem is large in proportion to the cap, very firm, often club-shaped. It's white to ochre in color with red-brown overtones. Look for the presence of fine ridge-like netting (reticulum) on the upper third of the stem. Neither cap, spores nor stems stain blue. The mushroom has a pleasant odor.

Cap: 3 1/2–10"

Stem: 1–10"

Look for fine white netting on upper stem.

Spore Print

| June | July | Aug. | Sept. | Oct. |

Habitat
Solitary to scattered on forest floors of conifer (pine and hemlock) and hardwoods (birch and aspen). Often hidden below the duff and leaf layer. Mycorrhizal.

CHOICE

King of Edibles
This choice edible is known worldwide. In Europe, it is the best loved and most sought after of all wild mushrooms.

Nearly Smooth-stemmed Bolete *Boletus subglabripes*

The lemon-yellow pores and stem and its warm-brown cap make this mushroom an attractive find.

The cap color ranges from yellow-brown to orange-brown or cinnamon-brown. The pale-yellow cap flesh is thick and firm. A faint bluing may occur when bruised. The small circular pores are bright yellow but with age, pores become duller and turn greenish.

The long, solid stem appears to be smooth, but a hand lens will show that the entire surface is covered with stiff, granular scales called scabers. Because the scabers are colored like the stalk, they are inconspicuous and easily over-looked. A distinct tangle of white mycelium often clings to the base.

Another bolete with nearly identical field characteristics is called Jana's Bolete, *Boletus sphaerocystis*. Comparative microscopic study is required to distinguish the two. This bolete is commonly picked in Northern

Wisconsin. Like *B. subglabripes*, Jana's Bolete is a good edible.

Habitat
In stands of birch, aspen and oak. Mycorrhizal.

Cap: 1 1/2–4"

CHOICE

Stem: 2–4"

| July | Aug. | Sept. | Oct. |

Nearly Smooth-stemmed Bolete

The Boletes

Boletaceae *or boletes are mushrooms that hold their spores under the mushroom cap in small tubes instead of on gills. Nearly as widely distributed as gilled mushrooms, they include the famous King Bolete.*

Boletes are a relatively safe group of mushrooms for the table (none are known to be deadly to adults). They are especially suitable for novice mushroom hunters, since there's little danger on confusing them with really dangerous mush-rooms, like the

Bolete pores

poisonous Amanitas. They are easily distinguishable from other fungi by virtue of their pores (and therefore lack of gills), and their thick stems and caps.

Some of the boletes are regarded as culinary delicacies, especially the King Bolete (Boletus edulis). It's generally considered to be one of the tastiest culinary mushrooms that can be found on the forest floor.

Two-colored Bolete *Boletus bicolor*

This is a robust mushroom that, as its name implies, sports two colors—its cap and stem are an attractive rose-red to deep red but both the pore surface and inner flesh is bright yellow.

The thick cap is smooth and dry. On young specimens you may find the surface covered with a velvety nap and there may be hints of yellow at the margin. Pores are small and angular with very short tubes. The pores discolor with age becoming olive tinted.

Like the cap, the thick, smooth stem is deep red or rose-red. An area of bright yellow is often visible at the stem apex.

A slow, weak bluing reaction may occur on any part of the mushroom when cut or bruised. The slowness of the bluing and its rather fleeting nature set this bolete apart from similar boletes where bluing is more immediate and lasting.

The blue-green staining reaction when the stem is cut or bruised can take a minute or two.

Habitat
Under hardwoods, particularly oak. Mycorrhizal.

CHOICE

2–6" wide

T w o-colored Bolete

Spore Print

Stem: 2–4"

| July | Aug. | Sept. | Oct. |

Russell's Bolete

The eye-catching feature of this mushroom is its crazy stem; the entire dull-red outer surface is covered by a mix of irregular, ragged ridges and deep furrows. The stem is long and thin and often curved at the base. It is firm and tough. Under moist conditions, you can find a sticky viscid area at the stem base.

The medium to large cap is rounded with a strongly down-turned margin. It varies in color; buff-brown, yellow-brown to wine-brown. The surface is smooth and velvety at first, and then breaks into numerous tufted patches. The yellow flesh of the cap is visible below the cracks. Pores on the cap underside are yellow, large and angular, almost maze-like. They are depressed around the stem. They stain a bright yellow if pressed or cut. Eventually, the pores become olive.

Habitat
Under oaks and other hardwoods, occasionally in coniferous woods. Mycorrhizal.

Boletellus russellii

Cap: 1–5"

Russell's Bolete

Also appropriately referred to as Jagged-stemmed Bolete.

Stem: 4–8"

Spore Print

July | Aug. | Sept.

Russell's Bolete

Dotted-stem Suillus *Suillus granulatus*

Mushroom pickers like this species as it is plentiful for a considerable length of time. The thick cap is broadly rounded at first, then flatter at maturity. It is smooth to wavy and when moist is decidedly slimy. Color ranges from honey-brown, to cinnamon-brown or rust-brown and the cap surface is often mottled and streaked with pinkish-brown tones. The pale-yellow flesh of the cap is soft.

The pore surface is initially white to pale yellow, but takes on olive tones with age. The small round pores are arranged radially from stem to cap edge and are often beaded with droplets of milky fluid.

The pale-yellow stem is cylindrical and solid. There is no ring. Stem top is bright yellow and interior is white. The notable feature of the stem is its decoration; much of the surface is covered with conspicuous pinkish to brown dots.

Habitat
Under pine, hemlock and spruce. Mycorrhizal.

CHOICE

Cap: 2-6"

The cap's skin (cuticle) can be readily peeled away making for easy preparations for table use.

Dots speckling the stem are responsible for both the common and Latin names (granulatus= granules).

Stem: 2–4"

Spore Print

Mycorrhizal with Eastern White Pine.

Dotted-stem Suillus

Hollow-stemmed Suillus *Suillus cavipes*

Where Tamaracks flourish, you can expect a fall fruiting of this hollow-stemmed mushroom.

In hand, it is pleasingly neat and attractive with a dark cap, contrasting yellow pore surface and sturdy dark stem. The cap is rich cinnamon-brown to tawny, convex then flat with a pyramid-like central hump. Its thin margin is down-turned and often hung with wispy veil remnants. Hairy, yellow-tipped scales cover the cap surface creating a soft, suede-like texture. Cap flesh is yellow and shows no bluing when injured. The large, sharp-angled pores are arranged in lines radiating from the stem.

The firm, straight stem may have a somewhat swollen base and is circled by a frail ring of veil tissue. The stem is yellow above the ring and darker below. Note that the lower portion of the stem of mature specimens is hollow; this is an important identifying feature.

Habitat
In bogs and low areas always with Tamarack, singly and in small scattered colonies. Mycorrhizal.

If the stem's base of a mature S. cavipes isn't hollow, it isn't a Hollow-stemmed Suillus!

Cap: 1¹/₂–4"

Stem: 1–3"

Note the angular pores.

Hollow-stemmed Suillus

Spore Print

White Pine Bolete *Suillus americanus*

If it's not under Eastern White Pine, it's probably not this species. A very common yellow-capped mushroom that is found in moss and lichen beds in white pine stands.

The cap is flat with a low central knob; the margin has scattered patches of soft red-brown hairs.

Spore Print

A flimsy, pale-yellow veil covers young pores, then breaks to form a curtain along the margin rim. The pore surface is a dingy mustard-yellow, with large angular pores that are elongated radially. They run a short way down the stem.

A spindly, but tough stem supports the cap. The entire surface of the stem is speckled with persistent, sticky, red-brown dots (glandular dots). The stem base is attached to the soil by white or brown cords of mycelium. When you handle this mushroom and its kin, your fingers will stain brown.

July	Aug.	Sept.	Oct.

Habitat

Single to gregarious under Eastern White Pines. Often comes up through dense beds of mosses, lichens and pine needles. Mycorrhizal.

The slimy/sticky cap has given rise to the colorful common name: Chicken-fat Suillus

◄── Cap: 1-4" ──►

Stem: 1 1/8–3 1/2"

White Pine Bolete

Slugs and Mushrooms

It is startling and disappointing when a fine looking edible mushroom turns out to be invaded by a troop of slimy, brown-bodied slugs. The first reaction is to toss the mushroom aside and wander on for better picking. But really, if we take time to look at their form and features, the mushroom munching critters are intriguing.

Our air-breathing slug is a mollusk, but with no protective shell. Its canoe-shaped body is flexible and stretchable (can stretch to 20-times its normal length!) which enables it to glide along smoothly, to squeeze through narrow openings and to climb stems. Upper tentacles on the head bear eyes, lower tentacles provide for taste and smell. The slug mouth is equipped with a rasp for grating food.

Slugs move along on a path of mucus laid down by their foot gland. These paths create a guiding network that leads to favored food. Most slugs are generalists, eating a broad spectrum of leaves, lichens, molds, decaying vegetation and, yes, mushrooms. While slugs are considered pests, they do play an important role as recyclers of forest debris.

Painted Bolete *Suillus spraguei (Suillus pictus)*

An eye catcher! At first glance, this bolete looks as if an artist took brush and paint to its cap and stem. The dry, yellow cap surface is overlain by conspicuous red to dark-red fibrous scales. And the yellow stalk, in harmony with the cap, displays a covering of the same reddish scales. The bolete's cap is rounded, then nearly flat. Its margin is hung with white, cottony veil remnants. The margin is down-turned initially, but becomes up-lifted and flared as the mushroom matures. Cap flesh is soft, pale yellow, and tends to stain blue or slightly red when bruised.

The yellow pores on the fertile surface are large and angular. They are radially arranged. The yellow stem is solid and may have an enlarged base. A gray, gauzy ring is found on the upper stem. Below the ring, there is a covering of red scales.

Habitat

Scattered or in groups under conifers, especially Eastern White Pine. Mycorrhizal with white pine.

Cap: 1¹/₂–4¹/₂"

Painted Bolete

Stem: 1⁵/₈–4"

Bright yellow pores under the cap are large and angular.

Spore Print

| June | July | Aug. | Sept. | Oct. |

Blue-staining Bolete

As its common name indicates, this bolete's blue-staining reaction to injury is immediate and intense. You can actually scratch your name on the cap and see it appear in deep indigo almost immediately.

G. cyanascens is a sturdy-looking mushroom with a straw-yellow, broadly-rounded cap that becomes depressed and flattened with age. The cap surface is uneven and made coarsely wooly by fibrous scales and mats of hair. The flesh of the cap is thick, rigid and brittle. The fertile underside shows small, round pores and is somewhat sunken around the stem.

Spore Print

The bolete's thick, stout stem is colored like the cap. Its exterior is dry and downy; the interior is stuffed with cottony pith. The stem is often swollen in the middle or at its base.

Habitat

This mushroom is found singly, scattered or in groups or dense clusters on exposed sandy soil and mosses under

Gyroporus cyanescens

second-growth hardwoods or mixed woods; also among rocks. Often along trails and roads. Mycorrhizal.

Blah in appearance—overall dirty tan—until you break a piece off. Within seconds the flesh turns a deep inky blue. Color change is very quick.

◄ *Cap: 1¹/₂–4"*

Stem: 1¹/₂–4"

| July | Aug. | Sept. |

Blue-Staining Bolete

Aspen Scaber Stalk *Leccinum insigne*

CHOICE

This bolete has a broadly-rounded cinnamon-orange cap with a somewhat grainy or fibrous surface that smooths with age. The margin of the cap over-reaches the pore surface and pieces of the cap cuticle (outer skin) hang down from its rim. The white flesh is thick and soft. Upon injury it stains lilac-gray, then almost black. The pores are dull yellow. The thick fleshy stem is white and has an enlarged base. Tufts of stiff, brown hairs (scabers) cling to the surface and gradu-ally turn black. The stem immediately stains violet to gray-blue when bruised or cut, not red as some look-alikes. The closely related *L. aurantiacum* slooowly turns burgundy or pink when cut or bruised.

◄ *Cap: 1³/₈–6"* ►

Aspen Scaber Stalk

Pieces of the cap cuticle (outer skin) hang down from its rim.

Stem: 3–4¹/₂"

Spore Print

| June | July | Aug. | Sept. |

Habitat

Scattered or in groups under aspen and birch. May also be under conifers (White Spruce, Jack Pine) in a mixed forest. Mycorrhizal.

Chrome Foot *Tylopilus chromapes (Leccinum chromapes)*

Caps are convex to broadly convex, dry, hairy to smooth, pinkish-red to tan. Flesh is white, pink below skin, not staining. Pore tubes are white to flesh-colored, aging brown. Pores are tiny and round. Stem is white with a pinkish tint and a bright yellow base, and covered with raised reddish dots. Like the Hollow-stemmed Suillus (*Suillus cavipes*) on page 76, mature Chrome Foot specimens also have hollow stems.

CHOICE

Spore Print

Habitat
Deciduous woods (aspen and birch) and conifer woods (pine and hemlock).

Cap on fresh specimen is dusty rose.

Note "scabers" on stalk.

Cap: 1½–6"

Stem: 2–6"

Stalk can be quite variable but the yellow base should be very obvious.

Chrome Foot

June	July	Aug.	Sept.	Oct.

Old Man of the Woods

The dark, densely scaly character of this mushroom makes it hard to spot in the leaf litter and wood debris it inhabits. Large, smoky-black shaggy scales cover the rounded to flat cap. The cap's basic grayish-white flesh shows between the scales. In young specimens, the scales are pyramidal; much like scales on an unopened pine cone. The cap margin is hung with a motley array of pallid gray

Cap: 1–6"

Stem: 1½–5"

July	Aug.	Sept.	Oct.

Old Man of the Woods

Strobilomyces floccopus

veil remnants. Pores are initially whitish. They are very large and angular. The tough, firm stalk has wooly zones made up of clinging pieces of veil. The portion below these zones is dark and scaly. All parts of the mushroom become reddish, then black, if bruised or cut.

Spore Print

Old and Moldy

The body of this mushroom is hardy; dry specimens can be found standing long after spore dispersal. Some remain intact so long that they become coated in green mold. No wonder the fungus merits the name Old Man of the Woods.

Habitat

Solitary to scattered in humus and well-rotted wood and leaf clusters among hardwoods (oaks) and conifers (pines). Saprophytic.

Chanterelle *Cantharellus cibarius*

You know it's summer when fresh crowns of Chanterelles push up to brighten pine needle beds and grassy woodland slopes. Everything about this mushroom is appealing. The cap is solid, smooth and a warm egg-yolk yellow. The white flesh is firm, but breaks crisply.

You may be wondering why this mushroom is not included with the "Gilled on Ground." But Chanterelles do not have true gills. Shallow blunt folds, colored like the cap, curve from cap margin to well down the stalk. These pronounced folds fuse and split in an irregular pattern. They have a fruity odor that suggests apricot.

The similar Jack O' Lantern (*Omphalotus olearius*, page 51) grows in clusters at the base of trees or on dead wood, stumps or roots.

Habitat

Scattered to clustered on ground under oaks and conifers; mixed woods. Mycorrhizal with spruce and pine and some deciduous trees.

A World Favorite

Chanterelles are known and appreciated worldwide. The French call it *girolls*, the Germans know it as *pfifferling* and in Scandinavia it is sold dried in packets for a camping soup mix.

The quantity and quality of its fruitings make it a target for commercial harvest. In the Pacific Northwest, this mushroom is a multimillion-dollar business.

Chanterelle

←Cap: 1½–6"→

Not true gills! These blunt and shallow folds form ridges that run down the stalk and resemble gills.

Stem: 1–3"

| July | Aug. | Sept. |

Morel (Yellow Morel) *Morchella esculenta*

One of the most popular edible mushrooms in North America. It is known for a tender texture and sweet flavor. The cap is rounded to bluntly cone-shaped and pallid tan to yellowish. The cap surface is composed of a network of interlocking round-edged ridges that surround shallow pits. This combination gives the morel a sponge-like or honey-combed aspect. The arrangement of the pale ridges is a haphazard affair with no set pattern. The small pits may be circular or irregular in shape with their interiors slightly darker than the surrounding ridges. The cap tissue bonds solidly with the top of a strong, whitish stem. The stem's surface tends to be slightly rough and granular and its stem base may be enlarged. The stem is usually shorter than the cap's height.

There's usually a single hollow chamber inside the cap.

CHOICE

M. esculenta is a wide-spread species and cosmopolitan in its choice of fruiting venue. It seems to favor lowland areas, but otherwise may show up almost anywhere—woodlands, old croplands, garden beds, orchards, excavation sites, riversides. Wherever it's

found, a meal of Morels promises to leave you delighted and satisfied.

Habitat
Varied; often near dead or dying elms, in old apple orchards, etc. (see sidebar). Saprophytic.

Cap: 1–4¹/₂"

Morels

Stem: 1–5"

| April | May | June |

Black Morel *Morchella elata*

Often the first true morel to appear in spring. Its dark cap is tall and narrowly conical. A network of brown-black ridges divides the surface of the cap vertically and horizontally forming and outlining the deep rectangular, yellow-brown pits (alveoli) where spores will develop. Pits may be irregular due to the path and curves of the ridges. Some longer ridges can be traced from one margin, up over the cap and down to the opposite margin.

Cap and stem are more or less a continuous unit, sometimes showing a crease where cap joins stem. The thick stem is cream-colored to dingy yellow with a surface roughened by a coating of fine granules. The enlarged stem base may be grooved and wrinkled. The interior of the entire fruiting

Cap: 1–3 1/2"

Black Morel

In most true Morels, the cap is attached to the stalk along the entire length of margin.

Stem: 2–4"

body is hollow. The mushroom has a pleasant odor. This is such a popular edible that troops of eager people converge yearly on possible fruiting sites hoping to find and harvest troops of morels.

Habitat
M. elata fruits alone or in groups under conifers (spruce and pine) and on sandy soils in mixed hardwood forests. It has been known to occur in very large numbers in areas recently burned. Mycorrhizal.

| May | June |

Morel Folklore

Morels are such a sought edible that a good batch of folklore has grown to pin-point their fruiting time. The advice is varied. Look for them—

- when first asparagus spear breaks ground
- when oak leaves are size of squirrel's ear
- when crocus buds unlock
- when lilacs and woodland violets bloom
- when Mother's Day comes round
- after lightning storm or late frost
- when the Cottonwood seeds fly

As to the matter of where to find morels, things become muddled. Lore favors stands of dead or dying elms and apple orchards. But suggestions from seasoned morel hunters cover a gambit of possibilities. Look where there's fire-scorched earth, where slopes face south, where black cherries grow. Check abandoned farm fields, stream banks, railroad right-of-ways, disturbed ground. It's even possible morels may spring up from the fill you packed around that new deck you just built or from soil spread in your garden beds.

The moral of all this seems to be, "Stay alert, travel promising territories, cozy up to successful morel hunters and always carry a basket just in case."

Conifer False Morel (Brain Fungus) *Gyromitra esculenta*

A very distinctive spring mushroom. The yellow-brown to bay-brown cap of this *Gyromitra* has a convoluted form much like a human brain.

The cap is lobed, thin, brittle and waxy. Its interior is hollow and chambered. The thick stem is pallid to buff with a smooth, faintly grooved surface and enlarged base. It has a simple or double chambered interior and, in young specimens, is stuffed with cottony fibrils.

Rocket Fuel Propellant or Tasty Snack?
Controversy swirls around the question of this mushroom's edibility. Many claim to eat and enjoy it without ill effect. However, scientific study of this species has revealed the presence of a carcinogenic toxin, monomethylhydrazine (MMH), used as a propellant for the rocket fuel in the Space Shuttle. The unpleasant symptoms of MMH occur two to twelve hours after eating, included headache, abdominal pain, cramps, diarrhea and vomiting. In severe cases, liver, kidney and red-cells are damaged. Fourteen percent of reported poisonings were fatal. But even if you don't get sick at first, the toxins may be cumulative and fatal over time. As mycologist David Arora puts it, "There is a narrow threshold between the amount of MMH the human body can safely absorb and the amount which can cause acute illness, even death. It seems foolhardy to risk eating a mushroom species containing MMH."

Habitat
Solitary or in groups on sandy soil, wood chips or disturbed soil. On ground under balsam, pine, spruce and sometimes aspen. Saprophytic.

Cap:
2–4" wide, 1–4" high

Stem:
1/2–3"

Conifer
False
Morel

May	June

Fruiting body is folded and wrinkled like a brain. One of its common names is the Brain Mushroom.

The False Morel's cap is not attached to the stalk except at the very top.

Saddle-shaped False Morel *Gyromitra infula (Helvella infula)*

Cap:
1–4" wide,
3/8–1 5/8" high

The head of this false morel is typically saddle-shaped. The brittle yellow-brown to red-brown cap has a smooth, undulating surface and a hollow interior. It is not deeply wrinkled or convoluted. Its inward-curving margin is partially attached to the stem and the free margin edges are often very wavy. Two uplifted lobes form twin peaks and create a cleft between them (the "saddle"). Some caps have three lobes and do not form the typical saddle. The stalk is soft and waxy with a smooth, or velvety surface. It is pallid with hints of pink or yellow. The interior is simple, unchambered and sometimes stuffed with cottony fibrils. Unlike *Helvella crispa,* this species is brown with a much smoother, more irregularly lobed stem.

Habitat

This species grows in soil rich in wood debris and well-rotted logs. Under both pines and hardwoods. Saprophytic.

July	Aug.	Sept.	Oct.

Saddle-shaped False Morel

Stem:
1–2 1/2"

White Elfin Saddle

Cap:
5/8–2 3/8" wide,
3/8–1 5/8" high

Stem:
1–3"

The cap's underside is densely fuzzy.

White Elfin Saddle (White Helvella) *Helvella crispa*

Pale coloration and fantastic form give this small mushroom a surreal, cartoon-like aspect. The entire fruiting body is cream-white with hints of yellow or pink. Stem is heavily ridged. The flesh is thin and brittle. When the mushroom emerges, the cap margin is rolled in over the fertile head. Gradually the margin unrolls becoming quite wildly up-lifted, curved and flared. Some say the mature cap resembles a saddle (hence, the name). The stalk interior is hollow and chambered.

Habitat

On grass and in coniferous and deciduous forests.

July	Aug.	Sept.	Oct.

Black Elfin Saddle *Helvella lacunosa*

The coarsely wrinkled cap is gray-brown to dull black. Parts of the cap margin are pressed against, or attached to, the stalk. Other cap lobes arch into double peaks that create a deep, saddle-like cleft. Cap flesh is thin and brittle. The sterile underside is gray-brown to black in color. The dingy white to gray stalk is quite a fantastic work of nature.

The surface is fluted (lacunose); double-edged vertical ribs run the length of the stalk and branch irregularly forming pockets and pits. A cross-section of the hollow stem reveals complex chambering inside.

Habitat

H. lacunosa is found on the ground in deciduous and coniferous woods.

Aug.	Sept.	Oct.

Cap:
1–2" wide
3/8–2" high

Stem:
2 5/8–5"

Black
Elfin
Saddle

◄— Cap: 2-6" —►

Scaly Vase *Gomphus floccosus*

This mushroom begins as a blunt cylindrical body. It gradually broadens to form a deep, funnel-like or vase-shaped structure. The inner surface is covered with coarse orange to yellow-orange scales. Scales lie flat at the mouth of the funnel, but curl and curve downward over the depressed center. The fertile sides have shallow, rounded wrinkles across the surface. It is pale ochre in color. The hollow stem—more or less an extension of the cap—is cream-buff above and has a white base. Fruitings of this fungus appear in groups under conifers or in mixed woods. They sometimes grow in fairy rings.

Habitat

Solitary, scattered or in groups on soil in conifer or in mixed forests. Saprophytic or mycorrhizal.

June	July	Aug.	Sept.

Stem:
2–4"

Spore Print

Scaly
Vase

Funnel Polypore (Tiger's Eye) *Coltricia perennis (Polyporus perennis)*

Funnel Polypore

This attractive stalked polypore often grows on sandy footpaths in conifer woods. The thin, shallowly depressed cap has a suede-like texture. It is patterned by narrow concentric bands of yellow, gold and varied shades of brown. The margin is typically paler. Cap flesh is rusty brown. Pores are large, angular and slightly decurrent. In mature specimens the pore surface is cinnamon brown. The cap is sup-ported by a sturdy stem that is velvety red-brown. At times, caps of several specimens grow together forming a multi-layered unit.

Cap: 1-4"

Stem: ⅝–2½"

Habitat
Found sprouting from sandy ground under conifers. Solitary or in groups along paths, roadsides, clearings and edges of burns. Saprophytic.

A polypore with a stem growing out of the ground? Yes, the Funnel Polypore is an oddity among the polypores.

| July | Aug. | Sept. | Oct. | Nov. |

May live for more than one year.

Leaves, sticks and needles are often incorporated in the fruiting body.

Wooly Velvet Polypore
Inonotus tomentosus (Onnia tomentosus)

Cap: 2-6"

A polypore with an upper surface that is dry and made velvety by a dense covering of hairs (tomentose). Its yellow-brown cap is circular to fan-shaped with a central depression and lobed, wavy margin. Faint, concentric bands of colors are visible especially near the margin. A vertical cut through the cap reveals two layers of flesh; the top layer is soft and pliable, the lower layer fibrous and sturdy.

The pores are often angular and in age tear, becoming tooth-like. The dark, rusty-brown stem may be attached centrally or laterally.

Spore Print

Habitat
Fruits on the ground, probably from buried conifer roots and conifer debris. It is also found on the trunks of living and dead conifers, especially pine and spruce. Grows singly or in groups, often with neighboring individual caps fused together at the margins.

| Aug. | Sept. | Oct. |

Wooly Velvet Polypore

Hedgehog Mushroom
Hydnum repandum

Most common of the toothed mushrooms. Resembles a gilled mushroom from above but a peek below the cap reveals a plethora of spines hanging down like tiny stalactites. The cap is flattish and yellow to brown with a wavy edge.

The Hedgehog bears its spores on the outside of the tooth-like spines, or "teeth."

Habitat
Solitary, scattered or gregarious under mixed woods, often near oaks. Saprophytic or mycorrhizal.

Cap: 1-4"

Spines recede as they begin to descend the stem, quickly disappearing.

Hedgehog Mushroom

Stem: 1¹/₂–6"

Spore Print

| July | Aug. | Sept. | Oct. |

Bleeding Tooth (Strawberries & Cream)
Hydnellum peckii

A strange toothed fungus whose cap surface is velvety and very irregular with pits, ridges and odd horny projections, often incorporating needles. The young cap is white to pink, and when fresh and moist, exudes dark red droplets which cling to the cap surface; this is the "blood" in Bleeding Tooth.

As the mushroom matures the cap becomes smoother and brown to dark red-brown. The margin, however, remains white to pinkish and is beaded with red droplets. Flesh of both the cap and stem is leathery to corky with faint zoning of pink-buff, cinnamon-brown and dark red-brown. The stem—

Cap: 1-6"

Bleeding Tooth

Stem: 1–3"

| Sept. | Oct. |

The "teeth," which are often hidden beneath the irregular cap, extend down the stalk.

usually hidden in the needle duff—has short crowded spines. They are dull pink, later brownish, with paler tips. This mushroom has a fragrant or pungent odor.

The similar *H. pineticola* also grows under pines but has more pinkish droplets.

Habitat
Solitary, scattered or gregarious in fused clusters. On the ground under conifers. Mycorrhizal with pines and spruces in woods.

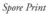

Spore Print

Common & Green-capped Jelly Babies
Leotia lubrica & Leotia viscosa

Dense clusters of *Leotia* are a fascinating find. Each slimy fruiting body is rather spike-like with a slender, compressed stem and a small slightly wrinkly and lobed head. They are rubbery and a bit translucent. There are no gills or pores, as the spore development takes place on the surface of the fungus head. Lifting a clump of these small mushrooms brings along sand grains, moss and woody debris bound together by strands of mycelium. There are

Cap: 1/2–2 1/2"

Spores are produced on the outer surface of the fungus.

Stem: 1/2–2 1/2"

Green-capped Jelly Baby

Common Jelly Baby

Cap and stem of new jelly babies are slimy. Stem may be filled with "jelly."

Cap: 1/2–1 1/2"

Stem: 1/2–1 1/2"

two species commonly encountered. *L. lubrica* is an all yellow-ochre to olive mushroom. The other, *L. viscosa*, differs in having a deep-green head. They are both stuck with the silly moniker, Jelly Baby.

Habitat

Found in mixed woods, scattered or in groups or clusters (clumps of 50 or more) on soil, duff, leaf litter or mosses, or on very rotten wood. Saprophytic.

July	Aug.	Sept.	Oct.

Jellied False Coral
Tremellodendron pallidum

Coral-like with several or many upright flattened and fused tips. Tougher than true corals, and leathery. Branches are more flattened. It is classified as a jelly fungus because of its spores. Unlike most coral fungi, *T. pallidum* has a longish stem and grows on the ground.

Habitat

Solitary, scattered or in groups on ground in mixed or deciduous woods. Saprophytic.

Fungi: 2–4"

Jellied False Coral

July	Aug.	Sept.	Oct.	Nov.

Dead Man's Fingers *Xylaria polymorpha*

Okay, some fungus names are silly—"Witches Butter" for example—but this one is dead on…excuse the pun. Clusters of gray-black *Xylaria* protrude grotesquely from the leaf litter looking like the decomposing fingers of a human hand, and thus, the macabre name, "Dead Man's Fingers."

When young and developing, this fungus looks more like "Dead Man's Nose," pale, short and rounded.

The clubs are blunt at the tip and are supported at the base by a short, cylindrical stalk. Clubs have a very hard exterior and are often twisted and distorted. The inner flesh is white, fibrous and tough. The club is basically a mass of fungal tissue (*stoma*) that houses flask-like spore-producing organs. The ends of the tiny "flasks" (*perithecia*) pierce the outer skin of the club and give it a pimpled, roughened look. The fungus fruits whitish in early summer and by late summer becomes blackish.

Spores are produced on miniscule organs that pierce the outer crust of the fungus.

Habitat

Clubs are usually found at soil level attached to below-ground rotting deciduous wood. They tend to grow in clusters near rotting beech, maple, elm, birch or basswood. Saprophytic.

Dead Man's Fingers

Fungus: 3/4–2 1/4"

3/4" wide

Mushrooms start out more whitish but turn blackish later in the season.

June	July	Aug.	Sept.	Oct.

Yellow Fairy Fan
Spathularia flavida

It is a delight to find a colony of these small fungi carpeting a patch of pine woods. Their design is whimsical, suggesting a dainty, lady's hand fan. The cream-yellow upper part of the mushroom is flattened and spread in the form of a fan or spatula. Its surface may be smooth or wrinkled and is often lobed. The outer edges run down the stem on opposite sides.

Yellow Fairy Fan

Cap: 1/4–1 1/4"

Fungus: 1/4–4"

Look for clusters of Yellow Fairy Fan in pine forests.

The pallid stem is usually tapered upward and threads of white or yellow mycelium are found at the base.

Habitat
Needle duff in pine forests.

Strap-shaped Coral

Fungus: 1–4"

Strap-shaped Coral *Clavariadelphus ligula*

The fruiting body is typically a simple, upright, unbranched club. It is rounded at the top and somewhat flattened or spindle-shaped. The club surface may be smooth, wrinkled or shallowly grooved. It narrows downward to a small, hairy base, which often has mycelial threads holding to the surrounding humus. The color of the fruiting bodies varies: salmon-buff, brown or yellow-buff. The interior of the club is white and somewhat spongy.

Habitat
This fungus produces large numbers of fruiting bodies, scattered or clustered, where there is a moist carpeting of pine-needle duff or other woodland debris. Saprophytic.

July	Aug.	Sept.	Oct.

Fungus: 1–5"

Purple Club Coral

Purple Club Coral (Purple Tongues) *Clavaria purpurea*

The smoky-purple to amethyst color of this delicate club fungus sets it apart from other small clubs. The fruiting body is erect, very slender and tube-like, with a rounded or somewhat pointed tip. The outer surface is smooth. The club's interior flesh is white to pale lilac and is quite fragile. With age the club becomes hollow. A whitish, hairy base supports the club.

This fungus fruits in tightly packed clusters or scattered colonies in wet, grassy areas of open woods.

Habitat
Groups or clusters (sometimes dense) on wet soil in conifer (spruce and firs) woods. Saprophytic.

July	Aug.	Sept.	Oct.

Yellow Spindle Coral (Golden Fairy Club)

Clavulinopsis laeticolor (Clavulinopsis pulchra)

Scattered stands or tufts of these dainty yellow to golden-orange clubs enliven moist, mossy humus-rich woodlands. The typical club has somewhat flattened sides, a rounded tip and is unbranched. The surface is often wrinkled and grooved. The inner flesh is pliant rather than brittle and is whitish or yellow in color. Each club has a stalk-like base that tapers downward. The color fades when the club is dried.

Habitat

Solitary, in groups or clusters on wet and mossy soil in woods. Saprophytic.

July	Aug.	Sept.	Oct.

Yellow Spindle Coral

Fungus: 1/2–3 1/2"

Crested Coral

Cluster: 1 1/8–3 1/2"

Crested Coral

Clavulina cristata (Clavaria cristata)

Delicate, finely toothed (crested) branch tips lend a special charm to this small coral. There is great variety in the form and shape of its fruiting bodies, but usually a slender, white base supports a densely branched structure. The slender branches are irregularly formed; some smooth, some vertically grooved or wrinkled. The upper part of each branch is flattened and the tip decorated with the crest that gives the coral is name, *cristata*. When fresh and young, the coral is pure white to pinkish white. It may become yellowish or gray-ochre in age. A fungal parasite often causes the base of the coral to blacken and the many branches may become flat and fused.

Habitat

Solitary to scattered or densely gregarious on ground in well-shaded woods: hardwoods, conifers, grassy areas. Saprophytic.

July	Aug.	Sept.	Oct.

Gray Coral (Ashy Coral) *Clavulina cinerea*

This erect, spreading coral fungus favors Jack Pine territory. It has a distinctive smoky-gray to lilac-gray color. A profuse jumble of short, irregular branches rise from a common base. Branches may be smooth to slightly wrinkled. Some are compressed, twisted and grooved. Their tips vary from pointed to blunt. At times, the base and lower branches will blacken due to the action of a parasitic fungus.

Habitat

Low, moist, mixed woods and conifer stands, especially with Jack Pine. Mycorrhizal.

Aug.	Sept.	Oct.

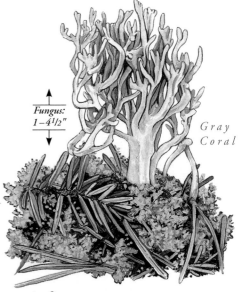

Fungus: 1–4¹/2"

Gray Coral

Cluster: 3–6", nearly as wide

Many-branched with "fingers" at tip and no "crowns."

Yellow-tipped Coral

Note the pinkish-orange stems with yellowish tips. But the pink tinge disappears quickly.

July	Aug.	Sept.	Oct.

Yellow-tipped Coral *Ramaria formosa*

The fruiting body is compact and bushy, with dense upright branching that rises from a solid, rooting base. The base is white below ground level. The pale branches may be tinted pinkish buff, salmon-pink or orange-pink. The white interior of the branches can be brittle or fibrous. The flesh bruises red-brown then blackens. Flesh is not gelatinous. Form and color of this fungus are in keeping with its name, *formosa* (beautiful).

This is one of a complex of nearly indistinguishable look-alikes.

Habitat

Look for it on humus-rich soils in conifer and hardwood forests. Mycorrhizal.

Veiled Stinkhorn *Phallus duplicatus (Dictyophora duplicata)*

This is the largest Stinkhorn in northeast North America. The mushroom's oval cap (or head) has a surface of branching ridges and deep furrows topped with a white-rimmed opening. Mature caps are swathed in a green-brown, foul smelling slime, attractive to flies and other carrion-loving insects whose activity helps disperse the stinkhorn's spores.

The white stem is long and tubular. Its body consists of spongy flesh made up of a multitude of small hollow chambers. At its base is a tough, egg-shaped volva. This volva is chiefly white but has some pale-brown coloration at its base. The lower portion of the volva is deeply pleated or grooved and is held to the soil by thick, pinkish-white strands of mycelia.

Head: 1 1/4–3"

Adding a touch of beauty to this strange mushroom is a pinkish-white veil that hangs just below the head. It is delicately netted and skirt-like.

3–7"

Veiled Stinkhorn

Habitat and Season
On the ground around hardwood stumps, on wood chips and in gardens.

June	July	Aug.	Sept.	Oct.

Dog Stinkhorn

For this strange fungus, life begins in an "egg." The oval egg is the immature button stage that has an inner gelatinous layer which splits to free the developing fruiting body. It remains at the base of the stinkhorn as a sack-shaped volva. The cylindrical stem that arises from the egg is pink with a slimy olive-brown spore mass covering the upper stem.

Stinkhorns start life as gelatinous egg-shaped structures.

The stem below the spore mass is covered by a network of minute chambers which capture light, and give the stalk an almost crystalline aspect. It is surprisingly beautiful.

It Stinks so Good!
The slime at the tip is foul smelling and sure to offend human sensibilities, but a host of flying and crawling insects find it very attractive and pay a visit, carrying off spores that cling to their feet and bodies, assuring wide dispersal.

Habitat
Solitary to clustered on ground or rotten wood in gardens, roadsides and woods. Often growing in needle litter, leaf litter, mulch, wood chips, humus,

Mutinus caninus

soil, decaying wood in coniferous and deciduous forests. Saprophytic.

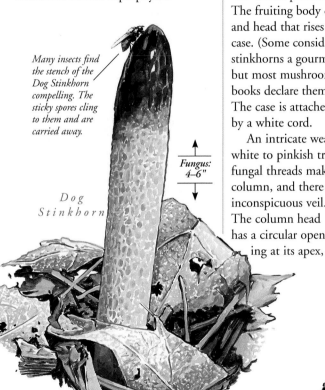

Many insects find the stench of the Dog Stinkhorn compelling. The sticky spores cling to them and are carried away.

Fungus: 4–6"

D o g
S t i n k h o r n

| Aug. | Sept. | Oct. |

Common (Ravenel's) Stinkhorn *Phallus ravenelii*

This mushroom garners attention with a powerful, off-putting odor. The fruiting body consists of a column and head that rises from an egg-shaped case. (Some consider "eggs" of such stinkhorns a gourmet delicacy, but most mushroom guide books declare them inedible.) The case is attached to the soil by a white cord.

An intricate weaving of white to pinkish translucent fungal threads makes up the column, and there is an inconspicuous veil. The column head has a circular opening at its apex,

Head: ¾–1¾"

and is covered with a thick greenish spore mass. This sticky mass is part of the mushroom's strategy for spore dispersal. Its carrion-like odor attracts scores of flies, carrion beetles and other insects. As they feed, the insects are pasted with spores which they carry off to new sites.

Habitat
Singly or clustered on wood debris.

| Aug. | Sept. | Oct. |

Stem: 3–6"

C o m m o n
S t i n k h o r n

Note sack-shaped volva—the "egg" from which the fungus developed—common to all stinkhorns.

Pear-shaped Puffball *Lycoperdon pyriforme*

Our most common puffball, *Lycoperdon pyriforme* is nearly round with a narrow, stem-like base. It is somewhat pear-shaped in cross-section. The outer skin (peridium) is white to pale-tan, aging rusty-brown. It is smooth with only a scattering of granules or spines on the top. This outer layer gradually falls off, revealing a smooth inner skin which will eventually split open, allowing the release of spores. The spore mass is firm and white at first, then green-yellow and finally, at maturity, olive-brown. The fruiting bodies of this fungus are often found pressed together in large clumps on rotting logs, sawdust and rich organic debris. Old weathered fruiting bodies may be recognizable into the following summer.

A feature of note is the conspicuous massing of white mycelial cords (*rhizomorphs*) that anchor the individual puffball to the wood, connect the puffballs to one another and spread through the host wood or debris bed. This is a good opportunity to get a good look at the rhizomorphs of a fungus.

Size: 1/2–2"

Young puffball

Mature puffballs: Note split in skin prior to release of spores.

Airborne spores

with stem: 3/8–1 1/4"

Pear-shaped Puffball

Habitat
Single to dense clusters on rotten logs or stumps, usually decaying deciduous wood, some conifers. Occasionally on ground rich in vegetable fragments. Saprophytic.

The Puffballs

Puffballs are round ground-hugging fungi that could be mistaken for stray golf balls. Most species have a whitish outer husk or shell with spines that slough off after a while. As the densely clustered spores mature inside the puffball into a powdery mass, a pore cracks open at the apex. Any raindrop, deer hoof, hiker's boot or child's poking finger hitting the dried shell will release millions of spores in a tiny cloud that really puts the "puff" in puffball. The wind does the rest, dispersing spores far and wide.

In young edible puffballs, the spore mass inside is firm and white.

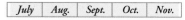

| July | Aug. | Sept. | Oct. | Nov. |

Giant Puffball *Calvatia gigantea*

It's a rock, a sleeping sheep, no, it's a Giant Puffball! Well-known and often eaten, this species sometimes reaches enormous size; specimens five feet long and weighing 56 pounds have been reported. Ordinarily though, the fruiting bodies are smaller, perhaps the size of a softball or football. The cream-white spore case is nearly round when young, but flattens and becomes oval as it matures (like a very large lump of dough that awaits kneading). The thick outer skin is smooth and much like kid-leather to the touch. The skin surface eventually cracks into plates of tissue that flake and fall away. An inner, olive-brown layer still encloses the spore mass until dispersal. Then, the protective wall disintegrates, exposing the spores (yellow to olive-brown) to the elements.

The Giant Puffball is stemless, but a thick, rooting mycelial cord attaches it to the soil. When white and solid inside, the Giant Puffball is an excellent and eagerly sought-after edible.

Habitat
Solitary or scattered in meadows, fields, gardens, cemeteries, along roads, edge of streams, parks and golf courses. Prefers good rich soil. Saprophytic.

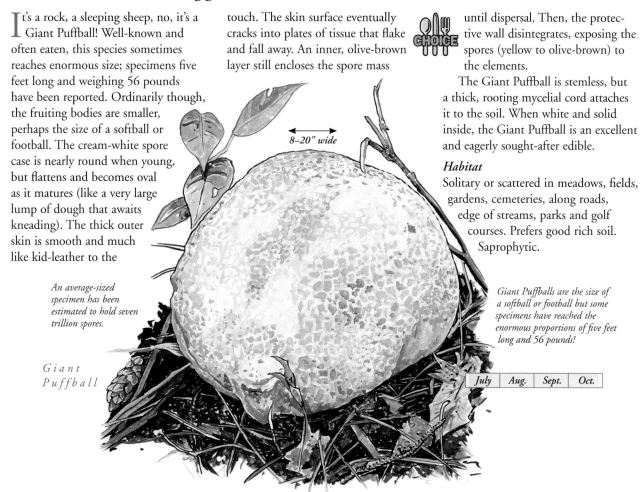

8–20" wide

An average-sized specimen has been estimated to hold seven trillion spores.

Giant Puffball

Giant Puffballs are the size of a softball or football but some specimens have reached the enormous proportions of five feet long and 56 pounds!

| July | Aug. | Sept. | Oct. |

Gem-studded Puffball *Lycoperdon perlatum*

Dense clusters of these puffballs can be found in open spots along paths, roads and in woodlands. The fruiting body consists of a round top and thick, wrinkled sterile base. The outer wall of the structure is pale-ochre to cream-colored. Its surface is covered by conical spines that add a decorative touch. The spines are gradually shed, leaving networks of open, bare patches across the surface (making it aerolate). The spore mass

Note cream-white interior—you may be able to eat this one.

inside is firm and white, but as the spores mature, it becomes soft and olive-brown. A hole develops on top of the fruiting body to release spores for dispersal. It seems a part of the human experience to have put a heel to some of these odd, ball-like entities eliciting an explosive puff of brown powdery dust, blissfully

2-6"

Note the conical spines covering the surface.

1–3"

Gem-studded Puffball

unaware, probably, that you were assisting with the dispersal of countless living spores.

Habitat
Clustered in open woods and grasslands. Growing on mulch, compost, humus and woody debris.

July	Aug.	Sept.	Oct.

Saprophytic.

Pigskin Poison Puffball (Earthball) *Scleroderma citrinum (Scleroderma aurantium)*

Cut this puffball in half and you will not find fine white flesh but rather a poisonous mass of purple-black spores. At maturity the shell cracks open irregularly—unlike the nice neat pore openings at the tips of other small puffballs. Scales on the outer skin each have a smaller centered

1–4

1–3"

wart with a polygonal background.

Does the specific epithet (*citrinum*) refer to this husk's resemblance to an orange peel? It looks much more like a grapefruit rind.

Habitat
Solitary, scattered or in groups on ground or decaying wood. On or near old stumps in wet spots in conifers and hardwoods. Mycorrhizal with deciduous trees.

Note dark spore body — watch out, it's poisonous!

Earthball

July	Aug.	Sept.	Oct.

Barometer Earthstar *Astraeus hygrometricus*

A small, globe-like structure made up of a thin, papery inner spore sac and a tough protective outer skin. The spore sac is whitish, becoming gray-brown with a rough surface. It holds a white spore mass, which eventually, as spores mature, becomes brown and powdery.
An irregular opening will develop at the top for spore release.

The unique outer layer splits star-like into blackish-gray rays, each decorated with a distinctive pattern of cracks. The base is attached to the soil by dark mycelial threads. The Earthstar responds to changes in the weather with a surprising bit of acrobatics. In dry weather, the rays close tightly, protectively, around the spore sac. On wet days, the rays spring open, bend back and lift the sac, exposing it to raindrops for an assist with spore dispersal. You can witness the earthstar action by putting closed, dry specimens on a plate and adding water. In a matter of minutes, the stars open and boost the spore sac up on curved rays.

3-4"

Barometer Earthstar

Habitat
Solitary, scattered or in groups in sandy soil, sand dunes, pastures, paths and roadsides. Dry open woodlands. Prefers sandy soils around the Great Lakes.

Sept.	Oct.	Nov.

Body may last all year

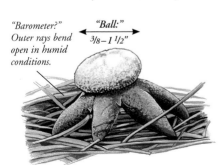

"Barometer?" Outer rays bend open in humid conditions.

"Ball:" 3/8 – 1 1/2"

Old Lumpy Potato?

Though odd in form and appearance (some liken it to an old lumpy potato), the **Dyers False Puffball (Pisolithus tinctorius)** has unrivaled value. Like many mushroom species, it establishes mutually beneficial relationships with the roots of trees and other green plants, helping to foster their growth and vigor. Dyer's False Puffball is known to have such relationships with more than 30 species of trees and is considered of such worth that an industry has grown up promoting production and collection of its spores. These are used in nurseries to inoculate pine seedlings to ensure healthy development and longevity. The spores are also introduced into garden soils to promote growth of plants and shrubs. In addition to such uses, this strange mushroom is a source of brown dye.

Cross-section

A nearly mature, dissected P. tinctorious reveals a new world: small, crowded, pea-shaped spore packets spread across the interior in a dense jelly-like matrix.

Scarlet Cup *Sarcoscypha austriaca (S. coccinea)*

Wander about the northern hardwood forests in the spring to search out the stunning Scarlet Cup. When the spring ephemeral flowers begin blooming, Scarlet Cup blazes from the shadows of last year's leaves. Brush away the leaf litter beneath a mature basswood or oak and you may find this treasure. Its fruiting body is a bright scarlet cup, shallow or deeply concave, with an incurved margin.

Spores develop within the cup. The pale underside is frosted by a matting of fine white hairs. The cup sits on a short white stalk.

Native Americans used the cups for medicinal purposes, possible as an antibiotic.

Habitat
Northern hardwood forests. Single or several on rotting branches buried in leaf litter. Saprophytic.

One of the earliest of spring fungi. Usually appears before the trees leaf out. Regularly seen with spring wildflowers on the forest floor.

Often buried beneath last year's leaves.

April	May	June

Cup:
← 1/2" wide and 1" deep →

Scarlet Cup

Bird's-Nest Eggs

The next two species are Bird's-Nest fungi, so named for their small egg-shaped forms in a nest-like bowl. So what are those tiny "eggs" in the Bird's-Nest fungus anyway? These nest/egg combos represent a bit of clever natural engineering. If you had an electron microscope, you would see thousands of spores in each hard-shelled "egg" or peridiole. The "nest" is simply a dispersal aid: each cup is designed so that the energy of an entering raindrop throws the spore packet violently outward, catapulting the eggs up to six feet! One related species (Sphaerobolus stellatus) can fling its spore case more than 15 feet!

In the case of C. striatus, each packet has an attached cord, which helps hurl it through the air with whip-like action. A special glue at the cord end attaches the packet to whatever it strikes. It might catch on shrubbery or grasses which are grazed by cattle or other browsers. The spores pass safely though the digestive system and are deposited where growth is likely.

Striate Bird's-Nest (Splash Cup) *Cyathus striatus*

The cup-like fruiting bodies are noticeable when grouped on dead wood, twigs and woodchips. They look like a bunch of miniature bird nests. A covering of coarse brown hairs gives the outside a shaggy look. Each cup has an inner chamber that is funnel-shaped with shiny, grooved, ochre-gray wall. At the bottom, are tiny dark packets of spores resembling eggs.

Habitat

Scattered or in groups on dead wood, vegetable debris in open woods; wood chips, twigs, bark, mulch under shrubs. More common during wet times. Saprophytic.

July	Aug.	Sept.	Oct.	Nov.

Striate Bird's-Nest

Nest: ³/₈"

¹/₄–⁵/₈"

¹⁄₂" wide and deep

Gray Bird's-Nest *Cyathus olla*

The "nest" of this small fungus is actually the fruiting body and the "eggs" are spore packets (peridioles). Outside of the nest is gray to brown and covered with very fine hairs. Inside of nest is smooth gray. The rim of the cup is wavy. It has relatively large eggs. They range from gray to black. At maturity, the top of the nest is ruptured and the eggs expand. Eggs are ejected from the nest by raindrops.

"Eggs" are relatively large: up to ¹⁄₂"

Habitat

May appear in clusters on a well-manured lawn, or on dung. Also found on soil, twigs, wood chips and even on old husks in cornfields.

Fruits July – November

July	Aug.	Sept.	Oct.	Nov.

Can be seen all year

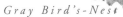

Gray Bird's-Nest

Orange Peel *Aleuria aurantia*

Who threw their orange peels on the ground? A fun fungus with a brilliant orange inner cup (fertile surface) and an outer surface made frosty and paler by a coating of fine white hairs. The cup is very thin and very brittle.

Cups in clusters, become flared and upturned from the pressure of their neighbors.

Carrot Color

The orange color of this fungus is chemically similar to carotenoids in plants. Sunlight is required for production of the color.

Habitat

Scatterings of these orange saucer-like fruiting bodies are found on paths, open woodland soils, and grassy roadsides.

June	July	Aug.	Sept.	Oct.

Orange Peel

3/8–3/4 "

Common Fiber Vase *Thelephora terrestris*

The upright fan-shaped caps of this mushroom are often found in dense clusters on sandy forest soil. Clusters may be 4 inches wide. They overlap and often fuse laterally to create vase-like formations. The deep-brown to fawn-colored caps are thin and leathery with whitish-gray margins. The upper surface of the cap is coated with stiff, lustrous hairs. Margins are ragged and irregular and bear a fringe of hairs. The cap underside is brown with violet tones. It is smooth at first or with shallow wrinkles. Over time, it will develop tiny wart-like bumps. The stem, if one is present, is very short and colored like the cap.

Tree Buddy

This mushroom plays an important role in mutually beneficial relationships with tree species.

July	Aug.	Sept.	Oct.

In the United States, *T. terrestris* is the most common naturally-occurring ectomycorrhizal fungus in forest tree nurseries. It has been determined that about 75 percent of forest-nursery tree feeder-roots are involved in partnerships with *T. terrestris*.

Habitat

On sandy ground or attached to twigs, roots and plant stems in coniferous and hardwood forests. Saprophytic and mycorrhizal.

Cap: 1–3"

Wrinkled, warty or smooth, its fertile surface tries to touch all bases.

Black Trumpet & Horn of Plenty *Craterellus fallax & Craterellus cornucopioides*

You need a sharp eye to spot a *Craterellus*. The dark-brown to black coloration of the trumpet-shaped mushrooms and their uneven, wavy margins camouflage them well in the beds of fallen leaves and woody debris that they like to inhabit. Once you find a group of *Craterellus*, you have an ID choice. There are two almost identical look-alikes—one commonly dubbed Horn of Plenty, the other, Black Trumpet.

Both are vase-like or trumpet-shaped with an open center that is hollow down to the small brown base that serves as stem. The cap is thin and fragile with a wavy, arched margin. The inner surface of the cap is smoky-brown to black. The outer spore-bearing surface may be smooth or wrinkled. Sometimes it is covered by shallow and blunt, vein-like ridges. Color ranges from gray to black.

Telling them Apart
Craterellus fallax often shows a hint of salmon pink or ochre at the rim of the trumpet and on the outside of the cap (actually a dusting of its own spores). *Craterellus cornucopioides* lacks any salmon or ochre tints and has white spores.

Habitat
Solitary, scattered or in groups in hard-woods (oaks, beech), hidden in leaves along old roads, trails and open places with mosses. Mycorrhizal.

July	Aug.	Sept.	Oct.

Horn of Plenty
Spore Print   Black Trumpet
Spore Print

⟵ ³/₈–3" ⟶

1–5"

Horn of Plenty
&
Black Trumpet

The mushrooms have a fragrant, pleasant odor suggesting apricot.

NON-GILLED *on* WOOD

Most of us are well acquainted with many of the species in this group. Who hasn't seen an Artist's Bracket fungus? If not in the woods then surely in a gift shop with a woodsy scene etched into the bottom pore surface.

Colorful blobs on rotted logs may be one of the small non-gilled fungi with the equally colorful names: Witches Butter, Eyelash Cup, Lemon Drops or Orange Jelly.

Some of our finest edibles are also in this group. One of the safest is the "Chicken of the Woods" or Sulphur Shelf that grows on oak trunks.

Many folks are curious about the rotting blue wood they find in wet forests. It is the work of Blue Stain, a tiny cup fungus whose mycelium stains its host wood blue-green.

And if it weren't for the non-gilled-on-wood gang, we would have precious little fungi to admire in winter.

Toothed Jelly *Pseudohydnum gelatinosum*

An intriguing little find that sprouts on very rotted conifer logs. The rubbery fan-shaped cap of this small jelly fungus is translucent, watery-gray, blue-gray or brownish. It is easily overlooked when tucked into the moist mosses on decaying wood where it grows. The cap can be velvety cream to brown and is smooth to slightly downy with thick flexible flesh. The fertile underside is covered by a multitude of tiny soft, translucent spines, looking like miniscule stalactites. A short stem holds

You most definitely need to get on your knees to appreciate this gem of a mushroom. Tiny translucent stalactite-like teeth are packed under the cap. This species is the only toothed jelly fungus.

the cap to the wood. It has the same gelatinous nature and texture as the cap. Sometimes the stem is absent.

Habitat
Solitary, scattered, or gregarious on rotting logs, twigs or stumps, especially moss-covered hemlock and spruce logs. Saprophytic.

Found on very well-rotted spruce or hemlock logs, often moss covered.

1–3"

1–2"

Flesh is rubbery.

July	Aug.	Sept.	Oct.

Toothed Jelly

Note translucence.

Lemon Drops *Bisporella citrina*

Hundreds of the fruiting bodies of this cup fungus can create a bright splash of color on downed hardwood logs. Green moss only accents the bright yellow cups. The tiny lemon-yellow cups are smooth inside and out and taper to a short, thick stem-like base. Lemon Drops may be scattered or densely clustered.

Habitat

In large clusters—sometimes in the hundreds—on barkless decaying logs, especially hardwoods: beech, oak, hazel, poplar. Saprophytic.

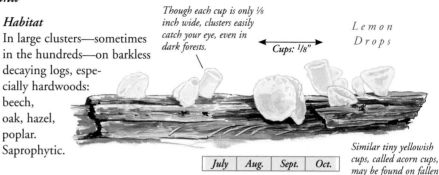

Though each cup is only ⅛ inch wide, clusters easily catch your eye, even in dark forests.

Cups: ⅛"

Lemon Drops

July	Aug.	Sept.	Oct.

Similar tiny yellowish cups, called acorn cups, may be found on fallen acorns or hickory nuts.

Orange Jelly *Dacrymyces palmatus*

Dacrymyces palmatus is a happy little fungus that will brighten any woods walker's day. The orange gelati-nous mass is found on decaying conifer wood. The mass is made up of flattened, irregular lobes of soft, pliable tissue. Orange Jelly is attached to the host wood by a tough white rooting base. The slimy mass eventually deteriorates, releasing the spores.

Mass: 1–2"

The rubbery orange mass of dense lobes fruits on dead conifer branches and stumps. The similar Witch's Butter is more yellow than orange and fruits on dead hardwood.

Orange Jelly

Butter Buddies

The very similar Witch's Butter (*Tremella mesenterica*) is yellow and fruits on dead hardwood. *Tremella foliacea* is brown and appropriately called Brown Witch's Butter.

Habitat

Dense clusters on coniferous logs and stumps; especially spruce. Saprophytic.

May	June	July	Aug.	Sept.	Oct.	Nov.

Eyelash Cup *Scutellinia scutellata*

Any fashion model would be lucky to have eyelashes as fine as those of this fungus. Black stiff hairs ring every cup. The small fruiting bodies are closed at first, but open to form shallow cups. The stalkless cups are bright vermillion to orange-red with a smooth fertile surface. The cups appear in clusters on rotted deciduous wood. A related fungus, *S. setosa*, is also fringed with black hairs, but it has a pale orange-yellow fertile surface.

Habitat
Mostly in woods; often growing in dense groups with mosses on decaying logs. Saprophytic.

Eyelash Cup

1/8–3/4"

| July | Aug. | Sept. | Oct. |

Blue Stain (Green Cups) *Chlorociboria aeruginascens*

You may occasionally come upon a blue-green log or scatterings of blue-tinted wood debris as you walk woodland trails. This unusual coloration is the work of a fungus that produces tiny cup-like fruiting bodies and bears the not tiny name of *Chlorociboria aeruginascens*. It is one of the few fungi known better for its effects on wood than for its fruiting body.

Once established in downed timber, its mycelium branches out and spreads through the wood, exuding, as part of its life processes, a blue-green dye. You are lucky if you find this fungus at fruiting stage with crowds of small brightly-hued caps. The fruiting bodies only emerge after a long wet spell.

Habitat
Mixed woods. Saprophytic.

The blue-green-stained wood is evident all year-round.

Blue Stain

1/8–3/8"

Fruiting bodies look like tiny cup-shaped growths with stems less than ¼-inch tall

| June | July | Aug. | Sept. | Oct. | Nov. |

Can be seen on decaying wood year-round.

Brown Cup *Peziza praetervisa*

Campers may find this small cup fungus occupying the campsite fire ring where it thrives on charred wood from earlier fires. The fruiting bodies are globe-like when they emerge, then gradually open to form shallow, stemless cups with wavy rims. The fertile inner lining of the young cup is purple to purple-brown, becoming brown with age. The cups may appear in clusters or as a scattering of individuals.

| June | July | Aug. |

Habitat
Scattered or in clusters on burnt ground and amongst charred wood in campsites fireplaces. Saprophytic.

Cup Cousins
Several other smooth brown cup fungi may grow here:

Peziza badio-confusa: on ground in woods.

Peziza repanda: on clusters of hardwood logs, humus, wood chips.

Brown Cup

Peziza badia: sandy soil, sawdust, under conifers.

Peziza succosa: damp soil in woods.

Devil's Urn *Urnula craterium*

What a perfect name for a jet-black cauldron of a fungus. In early spring you may encounter clusters of these urn-shaped fungi protruding from crevices in downed deciduous wood. It is one of the first fungi to fruit in the northern hardwood forests.

The dark-gray or brown fruiting bodies are tough and leather-like. They open up to reveal deep, black-walled cups where spores develop. The upper edges of the urn are typically scalloped or ragged. A thick stem supports the urn. It is dark in color and its base is surrounded by a mass of mycelial hairs.

Habitat
Look for the Devil's Urn on rotting hardwood sticks or rising from wood buried beneath the leaf bed. They often appear to be growing from the ground but gently pull away the moss or leaf litter to find the host wood.

2–3½"

1½–3"

Devil's Urn

| March | April | May |

Hen-of-the-Woods (Maitake) *Grifola frondosa*

You really need to use your imagination to think this huge clustered mushroom resembles a hen with her brown feathers flared and fluffed. But it does occur in the autumn woods, usually at the base of an oak. It is one of the largest of mushroom fruiting bodies in the North Woods, weighting 5 to 10 pounds or more. The mushroom is composed of a stubby, solid, many branched base and numerous, overlapping, petal-like or spoon-shaped caps. The leathery caps are smoky- brown. Their smooth or wrinkled surface is covered with tufts of minute hairs and there are faint color zones near the thin, wavy margins. Flesh of caps is white. Lateral stems attach caps to the branches below. Pores on the cap underside are creamy white, small and angular or maze-like. They descend onto the branches.

Cross-section view: note the common stem, dense branching and white-colored flesh.

Inverting the mushroom cluster reveals the white base, its dense branching and the light-colored pore surface of the caps. No part of this mushroom discolors when cut or bruised. It can be expected to fruit year after year in the same place.

Habitat
At the base of mature decidu-ous trees, particularly oak.

Sept.	Oct.

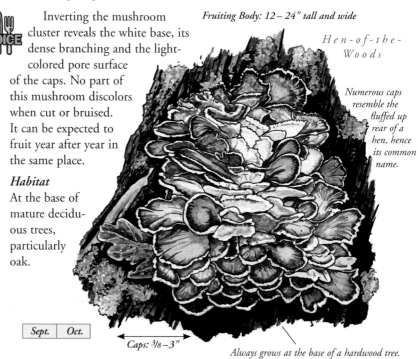

Fruiting Body: 12 – 24" tall and wide

Hen-of-the-Woods

Numerous caps resemble the fluffed up rear of a hen, hence its common name.

Caps: 3/8 – 3"

Always grows at the base of a hardwood tree.

Maitake Medicine?

This mushroom is prized in Asian traditional medicine. Maitake, as it is called in Japan, is utilized in a wide range of treatments that include regulating blood pressure, controlling insulin and glucose production, and reducing harmful cholesterol. There is, at present, research in the USA and elsewhere into its potential for prevention and treatment of cancers.

Tree Ear *Auricularia auricula*

Tree ear? The fruiting bodies, with their curves and lobes, create a remarkable likeness to the human ear. Groups of these odd fungi rise from rotting logs or hang on dead branches and twigs.

The shallow, irregular cups have a rubbery, gelatin-like consistency and a translucent context. The light-brown to red-brown sterile surface has a dense covering of silky hairs and is deeply ribbed and veined. Hairs appear as a whitish bloom on very young

May–Nov.

specimens. The slightly paler fertile surface is smooth to wavy and usually down-turned. Most of the fruiting bodies are stem-less.

Tree Ears are a popular ingredient in oriental cooking.

Habitat
Singly or in groups on conifer and hard-wood logs, dead twigs and branches. Saprophytic.

Birch Lenzites (Gilled Polypore) *Lenzites betulina*

Thin, leathery caps line downed logs, sometimes forming rosettes. Caps are semicircular or unevenly fan-shaped. They have a rough, grooved surface and typically display a series of narrow zones of color against an off-white background. These zones may be rose-toned, orange or shades of brown and gray. Presence of algae often adds a tinge of green.

The chief distinguishing feature of this shelf fungus lies on the underside of the cap. There you find white, gill-like

Underside showing the unique gill-like structures

structures. These are closely packed and consist of narrow, sharp-edged walls that radiate from the point of attachment and branch near the cap edge.

Ancient Chinese Secret
This mushroom has been used in traditional Chinese medicine. Modern study shows it has several medicinal properties—antioxidant, antimicrobial—and may have promise for those suffering autoimmune problems.

July–Nov.

Habitat
Chiefly on deciduous wood (not always birch!), occasionally on conifers. Saprophytic.

Presence of algae often tints the brackets green.

Bracket fungi

The following several fungi are bracket fungi, or shelf fungi, and belong to the family Polyporaceae. Notable for bearing fruiting bodies (conk) in a "bracket," these polypores have several to many individual mushroom caps that lie in a close planar grouping of separate or interwoven horizontal rows. Brackets can range from only a single row of a few caps, to dozens of rows of caps that can weigh several hundred pounds. They are typically tough and sturdy and produce their spores inside the tubes of the undersurface. Many types of bracket fungi are also polypores.

Examples of bracket fungi found in the North Woods include the Artist's Bracket, Sulphur Shelf, Tinder Polypore, Birch Polypore and Turkey Tail.

Hexagonal-pored Polypore

Artist's Bracket *Ganoderma applanatum*

This is one fungus that almost every person knows. Large, gray-brown brackets with an uneven crusty surface cling low to large hardwood trees. Some specimens may be nearly two feet across! The cap is zoned by a series of deep lines, ridges and furrows. The thin, blunt margin is white. The shelf interior is brown with a corky, woody context and seasonal layers of tubes. Pore surface is white and stains brown if bruised.

You will find many of the shelves covered with the powder of brown spores. Spores are carried from the pores to upper surface of the cap by wind or static charge. This may give spores an advantageous "launching pad."

Shelf Life

A shelf may live and be productive for as long as fifty years!

Perennial, year-round

Habitat

Found on nearly every species of decaying hardwood. It produces white rot in heartwood and sapwood of standing trees.

It's not called "Artist's Bracket" for nothing! Words or pictures scratched into the pore surface stain dark. Intricate designs can be inscribed.

Thanks for buying this book

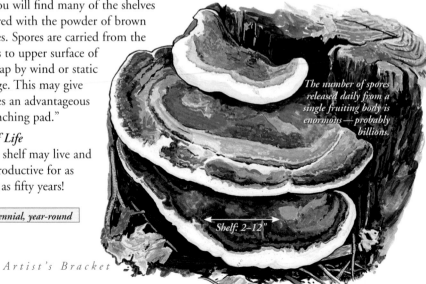

The number of spores released daily from a single fruiting body is enormous— probably billions.

Shelf: 2–12"

Artist's Bracket

Lacquered Polypore *Ganoderma lucidum*

The upper surface of the semi-circular to circular shelf is covered with a smooth crust, shiny as though lacquered. Color zones move from a central rich dark-red to a band of golden-ochre and then to a cream-yellow at the margin. The zoning is more prominent in some specimens and this, combined with the polished surface, makes them a very attractive species.

The inner flesh is soft, spongy and white in young shelves, but ages red-brown and becomes woody. Pore surface is cream, becoming yellowish with age. A stalk, if one is present, is thick with a varnished crust like the cap. It is suggested that dried shelves can be broken into pieces and steeped to make a healthful tea.

Lacquered Polypore

Year-round

Shelf: 2–12"

You'll only see the intense varnished reds, oranges and yellows in young specimens. These saturated colors will dull to a reddish-brown.

Habitat
Single or clustered on living hardwoods: maples and oaks. May also grow on stumps and roots of some other broadleaf trees. Saprophytic or parasitic.

Ling Chi

Forms of G. lucidum *that have a cap* AND *stem are thought to be the* Ling Chi *written about in ancient Chinese culture. It was documented in Chinese medical texts more than 2000 years ago. Among the 365 species of wood, grasses, herbs, furs, animals and stones utilized by traditional Chinese medicine,* Ling Chi *was considered of highest value.*

It was called "Herb of Spiritual Potency," or more mundanely "marvelous vegetable." It was said to have many beneficial qualities and was valued particularly to promote the body's resistance to disease.

In modern times it's been used in Asia to treat cancer and other diseases. Modern western science has begun to affirm the medicinal potential of elements in G. lucidum *to stimulate the human immune system. Research has shown that certain elements can be useful in controlling human conditions, for example: Peptide glycogen can decrease blood sugar and Triperene has been shown to decrease blood pressure.*

Hemlock Varnish Shelf *Ganoderma tsugae*

What you will first notice about this fungus is that the cap appears highly polished as though brushed with varnish.

Like its name implies, the shelf is shiny, appearing to have been varnished.

Hemlock Varnish Shelf

Shelf: 2–10" wide

Year-round

Found most readily on Hemlock trunks. When first emerging, it looks like a round knob.

This distinctive shelf has fan-shaped or irregularly rounded lobes that jut from hemlock stumps and logs. The uneven red-brown to maroon surface has a yellowish margin. Often attached to the wood by a sturdy, sometimes twisted, stem that shares the varnished look. Pore surface is white. It stains yellow or brown where injured. Always found on conifer wood.

Habitat
Hemlock and other conifers.

Red-belted Polypore
Fomitopsis pinicola

A striking polypore of decayed conifer stumps and logs, as well as the wounds of living trees. A semi-circular or hoof-shaped shelf with a crusty, resinous, red-brown upper surface and hard, woody interior. The glossy surface is furrowed and ridged concentrically. The cap margin is thick, rounded and creamy yellow. The white pore surface slowly stains yellow when bruised.

Apparently not a picky fungus; F. pinicola has been recorded on more than 100 different species of tree hosts.

Bracket: 2–15" across, 2–8" high

Year-round

The glossy lacquer-like sheen coating this attractive species will actually melt when a match is held to it.

Red-belted Polypore

Habitat
Solitary or in groups on logs and stumps of conifers, especially spruce. Saprophytic on dead trees; parasitic on live conifers and broadleaf trees.

Birch Polypore *Piptoporus betulinus*

Any mature northern forest with birch is certain to have numerous examples of these mushrooms on dying birch, birch snags and logs. The fruiting body of this fungus emerges from the bark as a rounded knob with the look, feel and consistency of a small rubber ball. The cap gradually enlarges into the familiar shelf-like form. The cap is kidney-shaped to broadly rounded, and smoky-brown in color. The cap covering is soft, easily dented and can be readily separated from the underlying white flesh. Young caps are elastic but firm, later the cap becomes hard and corky. The margin is blunt and rounded and projects beyond the pores to form a border. Pores are gray-white and round. With age, the pores dry, crack and become tooth-like. A thick stubby stem attaches the cap to the wood.

Fungus of Many Uses

P. betulinus, being such an abundant species, was noticed by early man and put to good use as a handy fire starter. It was also thought to be medicinally beneficial as an antiseptic. The famous prehistoric Ice Man discovered in the Alps had a specimen of this fungus tied to his belt. It was probably carried both for its antiseptic and fire-starting qualities.

Habitat

Restricted to trunks and branches of dead birch. Often in damp woods alongside *Fomes fomentarius* (Tinder Polypore). Saprophytic.

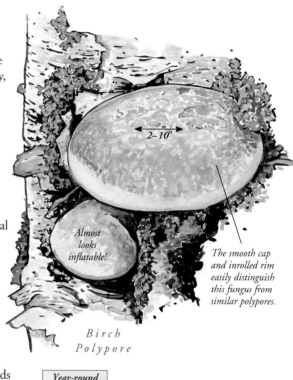

2–10"

Almost looks inflatable!

Birch Polypore

The smooth cap and inrolled rim easily distinguish this fungus from similar polypores.

Year-round

Yellow-red Gill Polypore *Gloeophyllum separium*

A striking, colorful display of semi-circular or kidney-shaped brackets, clustered, overlapping and often forming rosettes. The tough, stalkless caps are covered with a matting of stiff hairs. Distinct concentric ridges combine with radial wrinkles to create an uneven cap surface. There are bright orange to red-brown color zones with darker tones at the center and a lighter margin.

On the fertile underside, you find a curious maze-like combination of "gill" plates and large elongated pores. The "gills" are radially arranged and are often fused together. (Some specimens may have pores only and the pores sometimes become jagged or tooth-like.)

The maze-like gill structure of Yellow-red Gill Polypore.

Brown Rot

This fungus causes brown rot in both sapwood and heartwood of trees and may damage the woods in houses, docks, bridges fences and even telephone poles.

Habitat

Clusters found on dead wood including utility poles, fence posts, boards, bridge timbers, docks, railroad ties, slash, downed conifer logs and hardwoods: birch, hawthorn, poplar, cherry, willow, aspen. Saprophytic.

Yellow-red Gill Polypore

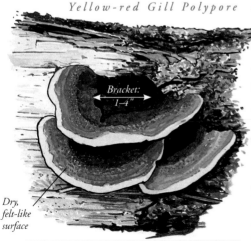

Bracket: 1–4"

Dry, felt-like surface

June	July	Aug.	Sept.	Oct.	Nov.

Annual to Perennial; may overwinter

Turkey Tail

Trametes versicolor

The name *versicolor*, meaning "variety in color," is a perfect fit for this fungus; no two are colored the same. Its fan-shaped caps sprawl along hardwood logs in overlapping shelves or form rosettes with cap edges joined. They are colorful indeed. Each cap is concentrically-zoned with contrasting light and dark colors including cream, beige, blue-green, orange and many shades of brown. In form and color, the clustered caps resemble the flared tail of a tom turkey and hence, the common name. The upper surface of caps has a silken texture and sheen. The margins are thin, waxy and sometimes lobed. The pore surface is white but yellows with age. Pores are

Cap: 1–4"

May to November

May last several seasons

Turkey Tail

very small. This mushroom causes white rot in the wood it inhabits.

False Turkey Tail (*Stereum ostrea*) is quite similar and may even be found on the same log, but note that its undersides are smooth and lack pores.

Habitat
Dense clusters on dead hardwoods and wounds of living trees in woods, parks and gardens. Saprophytic.

Papermaking and Turkey Tail

The paper industry employs several wood decaying fungi in the paper making process. T. versicolor is one of them. A major expense in paper making is the removal of brown lignin from wood destined for paper production. Scientists recognized that white rot fungi, with their specialized enzymes, could be a powerful tool in solving the lignum problem. Fungi like T. versicolor are used to chemically alter and bleach pulpwood, chiefly by degrading the lignin components, leaving the desired white wood cellulose.

Dryad's Saddle *Polyporus squamosus*

Large flattened, red-brown scales on the cap of this polypore lend it real character. The fibrous scales are concentrically arranged on the dry, cream-colored to yellow-brown cap surface. The cap may be circular or fan-shaped with a thin margin. It is often depressed and funnel-like over the stem. The white flesh is soft and succulent in young caps, but becomes corky and tough with age. The fertile surface has wide shallow pores that are irregular and angular. There is a stubby lateral stem darkened at the base by dark brown scales.

Spore Print

Found most commonly in the wounds of living trees especially willows, it is a parasite that causes white rot in the host wood. This mushroom also fruits on a variety of hardwood stumps and logs.

Habitat
Solitary or overlapping clusters in wounds of living deciduous trees, logs or stumps: elm, maple, willow, poplar, birch. Woods, along boulevards with mature trees, parks. Saprophytic or parasitic.

Cap: 2–12"

Dryad's Saddle

| May | June | July | Aug. | Sept. | Oct. | Nov. |

Sulphur Shelf (Chicken of the Woods) *Laetiporus sulphureus*

Note the radial furrowing.

A shelf fungus like no other; once you find it, you won't forget it. A yellow, rubbery knob emerging from the host wood signals the start of fruiting. But that's only a humble prelude to the quick development of multiple overlapping and clustered brackets with bright yellow-orange or salmon tops and intensely yellow undersides. Often, there are enough colorful

Shelf: 2–16"

Sulphur Shelf

brackets to occupy the entire side of a living tree trunk or solidly blanket a sizable log.

The caps are flat, semi-circular or fan-shaped with a thick, rounded margin which, in larger brackets is usually lobed and wavy. The upper surface has suede-like soft matted hairs. The fertile underside of the bracket is bright sulphur-yellow with pores so small they are barely visible without magnification. (Occasionally, a variety is found with a white pore surface.)

This showy mushroom has no dangerous look-alikes and the tender margins of the caps are a choice edible if harvested from hardwood. It has the flavor and consistency of chicken when breaded and sautéed or used as part of a casserole. On the other hand, some people have reported allergic reactions to eating and even to handling the mushroom.

One Old Oak

During a recent summer storm, lightning struck a 300-year-old Northern Red Oak that stood on the grounds of a North Woods resort. For several seasons, fruitings of Sulphur Shelf had appeared high up on the oak's trunk,

The pale yellow inner flesh is firm but succulent, much softer near the margin and tougher near the point of attachment to the wood.

now split and laid open. It was obvious that the fungus had been at work long before the orange and yellow brackets announced its presence; the heartwood was completely decayed and the hollow it left was tightly packed with baton-like masses of mycelium. Had it been spared the lightning strike, the oak might be growing today, still secretly harboring its fungal occupant.

Habitat

This fungus invades and attacks the heartwood of living trees. It causes brown rot that eventually hollows the trunk. Clusters of five to fifty grow on logs, stumps or trunks of deciduous or coniferous trees, especially oaks. May fruit on the same log for several years in a row. Saprophyte.

May	June	July	Aug.	Sept.	Oct.

Violet Tooth
Trichaptum biforme

This is one of the most common (and most overlooked) polypores in eastern North America. Violet Tooth is not as flashy as its larger cousins. It appears as multiple tiers of petal-shaped or semicircular caps. A bright violet tint can be seen on the cap margin. Caps are tough and flexible and remain leathery even in dry conditions. With age the coloring becomes uniformly white to buff. Pores are mauve in color and become tooth-like and jagged with age.

Habitat
On dead hardwood, especially birch.

Year-round

Look for the tiny teeth under the cap.

Tinder Polypore (Hoof Fungus) *Fomes fomentarius*

Annual growth rings are easily seen.

2–4"

Up to 4"

Check old Paper Birch trunks for this very common fungus. In shape, it resembles a horse's hoof. The outer surface of the bracket is thick-crusted and hard. The pore surface is ochre at first then darkens. Each year a new tube/pore layer is developed and the growth ridges are easily seen. It is a pathogen to living trees, causing white rot in both the sapwood and heartwood.

The Ice Man Carryeth

Ötzi trudging to his high-altitude fate.

From ancient times this fungus was used as a fire starter; the prehistoric "Ice Man Ötzi" found frozen in a glacier in the Alps, carried some in his leather pouch. The tube layers (pores) were soaked in saltpeter solution and dried to make a firestarter.

In early surgeries it was used as a styptic; shredded, the soft mass was applied with pressure to a wound, absorbing blood and encouraging coagulation.

Habitat
Solitary or in groups on decaying trees or logs; especially birch and maple, but may also grow on aspen, beech, cherry and poplar. Saprophytic.

Hexagonal-pored Polypore *Favolus alveolarus*

Distinguishing this mushroom is its rather large hexagonal or diamond-shaped pores under the cap. These cover the upper stem and radiate outward. This pore structure is very attractive and quite unique.

This is a common wood dwelling mushroom. The tough, thin cap is semi-circular to kidney-shaped. When young, its buff-red surface is covered with scatterings of reddish scales. The scales are eventually shed leaving a smooth cap. The flesh is white.

The cream-colored stem is thick, whitish, stubby and laterally attached. Some caps are stemless.

Also called Diamond-pored Polypore.

Habitat

Annually, on dead twigs and limbs of deciduous trees. Saprophytic.

Look under the cap for the distinctive hexagonal to diamond-shaped pores

Spore Print

Hexagonal-pored Polypore

| May | June | July | Aug |

Black Knot

These odd fruiting bodies are knot-like, black growths that clasp and girdle the twigs and small branches of living cherry and plum trees. They are a damaging parasite. The fungus begins as an olive-brown swelling and soon enlarges, ruptures and becomes blackened. During its two-year life cycle it elongates along the branch and encircles it. The fungal growth

Year-round

Surface is hard and carbonaceous, but flesh is white when young.

Black Knot

Mycelia embedded in the tree, often causes the affected branches to bend at the site of infection.

Apiosporina morbosa

interferes with the transmission of water and minerals and inhibits transfer of food produced by the leaves to other parts of the tree. The infected branches die and the tree is greatly weakened. In the second year, in early spring after rains, what is called a "shuck slit" occurs, opening the crust to release black fungal spores.

Habitat
Anywhere cherry trees live. Solitary. Several or hundreds on a single tree, clasping and enveloping branches. Grows on living cherry trees; especially Chokecherry. Parasitic.

Oozing Food
It is a fascinating fact, that the oozings of these ugly Black Knot fungal masses provide nutrition to a variety of feeding birds and insects.

Clinker Canker (Chaga) *Inonotus obliquus*

Looking much like the charred remains of a fire or a malformed pernicious canker, this crusty black mass is the initial growth stage of the Clinker Canker fungus. The black, hardened and deeply-cracked fungal fruiting protrudes from wounds in ailing, yet standing, birches and crevices in birch stumps. A seldom seen second stage bears the spores. It is dark brown, crust-like and grows closely attached to the wood. Pores may be circular or angular.

Chaga Tea
Though odd and unattractive, this mushroom has been a part of folk medicine for centuries. A tea called *Chaga* can be made by removing the woody conk, stripping away the black material and then boiling the yellowish interior. The tea is said to be rich in antioxidants and has been used to treat stomach disorders, consumption, and a number of cancers. Since 1955, Russia has approved its use in anti-cancer

therapy and the FDA has approved it as a safe nutritional supplement.

Habitat
Especially on birch; also on aspen, elm and alder. Parasitic.

Year-round

Chaga

Fungus: 10–16"

Grows relatively high on old birch and aspen trees.

Resembles a burl, a wound or a lightning strike.

Northern Tooth (Shelving Tooth) *Climacodon septentrionale (Steccherinum septentrionale)*

This large fungus is a woodland oddity. With its many overlapping gray-white caps jutting from a solid backing, it has the look of a misshapen unit of shelving. It resembles a polypore but it is not. The caps are sturdy with a hairy, uneven upper surface. Each cap is fitted with its own set of fungal dentures in the form of a tight crowd of short pale tooth-like spines that crowd the cap's underside. Though not a choice edible, it's been said that older dried specimens smell like ham. Yellowish-white when young, becoming tan with age.

Habitat
On standing Sugar Maples, sometimes beech.

July	Aug.	Sept.	Oct.

Northern Tooth

Cap: 4–6"

Clusters: 6–12"

Individual spines may be 3/4" long.

Bear's Head Tooth

6–12"

8–16"

Aug.	Sept.	Oct.

Bear's Head Tooth *Hericium americanum*

A thick supporting stem produces many stout, white, fertile branches. These branches divide repeatedly so that a firm compact structure is formed. Each branch tip has tufts or clusters of long, white hanging spines. These create a unique cascading effect or, as some see it, a likeness of a shaggy bear's head.

CHOICE

Fish-flavored Fungus?
One of the finest, most delectable wild edibles in the North Woods. Sautéed thoroughly, it is said to have a flavor reminiscent of fish. The real dilemma is whether to pick this beauty or leave it for other trekkers to enjoy.

Habitat
Look for this unusual mushroom on the sides of hardwood stumps and logs, sometimes in wounds of living trees: maple, beech, oak, hickory. Saprophytic.

Comb Tooth *Hericium coralloides (Hericium ramosum)*

An exquisite, pure-white fruiting body made up of long, curved branches that rise from a firm, rooting base. Branches fork and produce side branches to form a delicate airy structure. Branches are ornamented by tiny hanging spines arranged comb-like in rows along the entire lower surface of the branch. The entire body of the mushroom, aside from the tougher stem, is soft and has a pleasant odor.

Toothsome Treat

A delicious edible with no poisonous look-alikes. Cook it slowly!

Habitat

Found on decaying hardwood trunks, branches and logs, especially birch, maple and beech. It is sometimes hidden out of sight behind loose bark on snags. Saprophytic.

This is a detail of the spines. Like the Bear's Head Tooth on the previous page, the whole fruitbody is quite large: 3–10" across and 3–6" high.

Comb Tooth

July	Aug.	Sept.	Oct.

Name Game

The names of the Hericiums (ramosum, corralloides *and* americanus) *are still being shifted about, with various experts and authors applying names to different described species. All the ordinary mushroom hunter can do is look well at the specimen in hand, note its particular features, find the proper description and be aware that guides and texts may differ as to which of the three names is used.*

Crown-tipped Coral
Clavicorona pyxidata

A delicate member of the corals. Its fruiting body has multiple branches rising from a short, felty sterile base. The branches are attractively arranged in tiers with upper branches springing from the enlarged tips of lower branches (a candelabra-like effect). Tips of the outer branches are unique, each with a ring and small branchlets that together form a tiny crown. The body of the coral is pale yellow when young, but darkens and becomes brownish with age, especially in the lower branches.

Crown-tipped Coral

Habitat

This is one of the few corals that fruits on wood. It can be found on well-decayed hardwood stumps and logs, especially aspen, willow or birch. Saprophytic.

Clusters: 2–5"

June	July	Aug.	Sept.

NON-GILLED *on* OTHER

As in the Gilled-on-Other category, we have several parasitic species that mutate their hosts into completely new forms: "The Lobster" (named for its bright orange skin) and the Aborted Entoloma. They are quite common in the North Woods.

The tiny Pinecone Fungus looks like a gilled mushroom but has teeth under the cap instead of gills. Look for it sprouting from downed pine and spruce cones

Pinecone Fungus
Auriscalpium vulgare

Auriscalpium vulgare are easy to identify; you'll find these tiny mushrooms sprouting from fallen pinecones. They are a fuzzy tooth fungus with a myriad of tiny spines (or "teeth") lining their cap's undersides. The cap is attached laterally, not centered; late fall specimens may be more misshapen than earlier ones.

Habitat
Solitary or in small groups on decaying pinecones and maybe spruce cones. Also in needle litter and on branches in mature conifer woods. They have been found on corncobs. Saprophytic.

Cap: ⅜–1½"

Note the plethora of tiny teeth.

Stem: 1–3"

Aug. | Sept. | Oct.

Spore Print

Snow Mold
Typhula species

Circular patches of thread-like mycelia, three to twelve inches in diameter, grow on the dead grasses exposed from the melting snow. The mycelia begin growing under the snow. Fruiting bodies (sclerotia) are brown-black tiny clubs that grow on the dead grasses. Will only grow in sites where the snow cover is extended over about two months.

As the snow melts in early spring, dead blades of grass that were buried all winter are now exposed. The grass is damp from the snow melt, thus creating a small unique habitat. This is quickly taken over by a mold growth. So associated with snow, it is usually called Snow Mold (*Typhula* sp.).

Growing in open sites, the mold's mycelia begin under the snow and expand from there. Snow mold grows best in tempera-

Snow Mold

tures only slightly above freezing and once the grass substrate reaches about mid forties, it will no longer grow. Growing time is March and April.

Habitat
Dead grasses exposed by melting snow.

March	April

Lobster Mushroom *Hypomyces lactifluorum*

"The Lobster" is a curious phenomenon. A large, robust, white mushroom is overpowered and transformed by an orange parasite that seems to have less bodily substance than a coat of paint. This parasite constructs a crust-like mycelial cover that gradually engulfs the cap, gills and stem of the host mushroom, leaving only a hint of cap and faint ridges suggesting gills.

The gaudy orange crust holds thousands of tiny spore-producing bodies that appear as pimples on the surface and will eventually open to release spores. This parasite also changes the texture and make-up of entire host body. Large fleshy *Lactarius* and *Russula* mushrooms are its prime targets.

Habitat
Typically, the "Lobster" (parasite-covered mushroom) is found along pathways partially protruding from the soil, with humus and other debris clinging to its surface. Solitary or scattered on ground under conifers and hardwoods.

CHOICE

Size:
Usually 4–6"
Varies with host

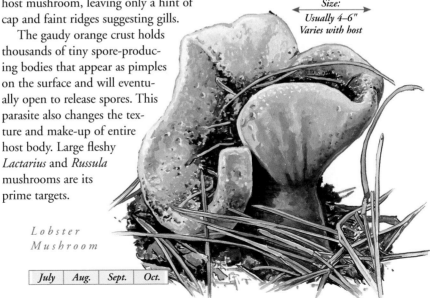

Lobster Mushroom

July	Aug.	Sept.	Oct.

Aborted Entoloma *Entoloma abortivum*

The aborted forms are rounded, lumpy white fruiting bodies. Some of them, fanciful observers say, are shaped like pig snouts. Inside, the white flesh is moist and soft. A pink marbling can be seen.

Aborted Entoloma

Aborted form: 1–4"

1–2"

Spore Print

Habitat
Several or in large groups in much-decayed or buried wood, around stumps or rotten woods, decaying logs; under hardwoods. Saprophytic.

Honey, I Aborted the Mushroom!
A strange kind of fungal combat is responsible for producing these odd whitish masses, the aborted mushroom forms found in humus near rotting stumps. One combatant is the small, all-gray mushroom with pink spore print called *Entoloma abortivum*. The other is the Honey Mushroom, *Armillaria mellea*. Just now scientists are pondering the relationship of the two. For years it was thought that the lumpy, soft masses of tissue were ill-formed *E. abortivum* infected by the Honey. Lately, it has been seen the other way around. The aborted forms are thought to be Honeys infected by *E. abortivum*. May the best researcher win.

The non-aborted form of Entoloma abortivum.

| Aug. | Sept. | Oct. |

FUNGUS LOOK-ALIKES

With no chlorophyll, fungi are usually not green and appear to be easy to discern from flowering plants. Though formerly classified as a type of plant, fungi are now put in their own kingdom. Not only do they not have chlorophyll, fungi also are devoid of leaves, flowers, seeds and veins within the stems. And yet, sometimes we can confuse fungi with flowering plants.

The North Woods is home to several species of flowering plants that live as saprophytes or parasites and so do not have chlorophyll. Best known of these is the Indian Pipe (Monotropa uniflora). Common in the mid summer woods, they are often associated with and growing in a symbiotic relationship with nearby trees. No chlorophyll means that the plant appears white and sometimes is confused for a fungus. A close cousin, not as frequent in the area, is also growing in the northern forest. Pinesap (Monotropa hypopithys) is more yellowish and flowers in a cluster; usually growing under pines.

The Giant or Woodland Pinedrops (Pterospora andromedea) is also without chlorophyll. Plants grow one to three feet tall

in dry soil among conifers where they are parasitic on pine roots. The dark to reddish stems hold many small bell-shaped flowers with tiny scale-like leaves.

Frequently seen under beech trees where live as parasites on their roots, Beechdrops (Epifagus virginiana) are usually brown. With small leaves and white flowers, the plants grow up to a foot tall.

Perhaps the strangest look flowering plant of the North Woods that could be confused for a fungus is the American cancer-root or squaw-root (Conopholis americana). Nearly six inches tall, the pale brown to yellowish plants are composed of a stout unbranched stem along with numerous scaly fleshy leaves. The tightly packed growths can give the appearance of light-colored cones growing from the forest floor. In dry woods, they grow mostly among oaks.

Although they are composed of fungi and algae living in a symbiotic (mutualistic) relationship, lichens are classified separate from fungi.

Woolly aphids may be one of the more unique "false fungi." In late summer, thick

mold-like growths may appear on the stems of some trees (alders seem to be the usual choice). White with threads sticking up, they do appear to be a fungus growth. However, a close look would reveal some movement!; not likely with fungi. Woolly aphids get their names from this white hairy coat that they tend to have at this time. The insects are in a tightly-packed colony as they feed on sap. White materials, including threads, are sent out through their exoskeletons to give this hairy or mold-like look. Being very hairy, these aphids may survive until the snow season begins.

Indian Pipe (**Monotropa uniflora**) *is a wildflower that lacks chlorophyll and could be mistaken for a fungus.*

SLIME MOLDS

Slime Molds are not fungi, but often share their habitat and are seen in their company. Slime molds lead a hidden life for the most part. They exist as amoeba-like life forms called plasmodiums. They achieve locomotion by oozing through their habitat (soil, wood debris or other organic material) consuming bacteria or microscopic food particles as they go.

At fruiting time, the plasmodium moves to an exposed surface where wind and rain will help with spore dispersal. Once in place, the slime mold plasmodium undergoes metamorphosis.

In accord with its species, the slime mold may form into troops of upright structures resembling miniature brush bristles; it may form a blanket of white or gaudy colored material on stumps, forest debris or on soil; it may form small pea-shaped cushions on logs; or construct other forms, sometimes of fantastic design.

Blackberry Slime *Metatrichia vesparum*

This dark, reddish-black slime sheeting rotten wood gives rise to stalks bearing a group of tiny, oval, lidded fruiting bodies (sporangia). The bodies are maroon to black with a metallic shine. The lids are dome-shaped. Their brick-red supporting stalk is fairly thick and solid and is surrounded at the base by vein-like strands of tissue.

The clusters arise from a single stalk.

Sporangia

Stem: 1/16 – 1/8"

Eventually, the lids of the sporangia break open revealing a purplish-red mass, a mix of red threads (capillitium) and spores. Action of the threads helps expedite the release of the mature spores.

Habitat
Found on well-rotted wood.

Head: 1/16 "

The blue-black sheen of the clustered fruit bodies (sporangia) reminds one of blackberry bunches.

Blackberry Slime

| July | Aug. | Sept. | Oct. |

Chocolate Tube Slime *Stemonitis* species

A shining base sheet gives rise to multiple fruiting bodies with elongated, cylindrical tops and short polished black stems. These sporangia form closely-packed erect clusters on a common base. They look like tufts of miniature brush bristles as they range here and there along the host wood. The purple black spores break out of the cylinders at maturity.

Common name refers to the stalked spore-bearing cases pictured below. The plasmodium stage is a white mass.

Habitat

Dead wood, downed logs in woods.

Wonderful common names for this fungus include Chocolate Tube Slime *and* Pipecleaner *slime. How about "Fudgecicle Slime?"*

Cap: $^1/_{32}$–$^1/_{16}$"

These cylindrical brown structures are the sporangia.

Stem: $^1/_8$–$^1/_4$"

Chocolate Tube Slime

July	Aug.	Sept.	Oct.

There are several species of Stemonitis *that can only be identified by microscopic structures.*

Red Raspberry Slime
Tubifera ferruginosa

A slime that will stop you in your tracks. When young, these sporangia are beautiful. They are bright rose-red, almost

Each fruiting body: $^1/_{16}$" *wide,* $^1/_8$–$^1/_4$" *high*

An opening at the top of the fruiting body allows release of spores when they are ready for dispersal.

Older, spore-producing bodies.

Younger fruiting bodies.

The tubes age from bright pinkish-red to brownish-gray.

Red Raspberry Slime

iridescent, and standing in a cluster, may resemble a multi-petaled flower head. Some groupings press into large cake-like formations. The transparent slime base produces tight crowds of cylindrical to oval fruiting bodies. As the sporangia mature, they leave beauty behind and become a dull purple-brown. The spore mass inside is yellow-brown. Also known as Pink Slime or Rose-red Slime.

Habitat

This slime mold is found on well-rotted logs or leaf litter, often with mosses.

June	July	Aug.	Sept.	Oct.	Nov.

Tapioca Slime *Brefeldia maxima*

One of the largest of the slime molds, it spreads widely over the host forming a shiny silver base for its cushion-like groups of sporangia. The mound of young fruiting bodies is white to off-white and has the look of a spill of thick tapioca pudding. As the sporangial mass matures, it becomes pink tinged and finally purple-brown and crust-like. Brownish-purple black spores are released when the outer crust crumbles and breaks away. Found on dead wood and living plants.

Habitat

May fruit on living or dead wood.

A giant among slime molds. The large glob of tapioca-like slime may be 12 inches across!

Mass: 1 1/2-12" wide, 1/4–5/8" thick

Common name comes from the young form (plasmodium), which is white and lumpy. As the blob ages it turns black and crusty eventually bursts to release a mass of brown/black spores.

Tapioca Slime

July	Aug.	Sept.	Oct.	Nov.

Scrambled Egg Slime *Fuligo septica*

This eye-catching slime mold forms irregular, spongy masses that spread across rotting wood and beds of decaying plant materials. It often invades composted garden beds. Its texture and strong ochre-yellow to off-white color move some to give it the unflattering moniker "dog vomit slime." As slime molds do, it first moves in amoeba-like fashion, engulfing nutrients including bacteria and organic matter. Finally it migrates to a favorable spot for spore dispersal and forms its characteristic soft, yellow mounds. At maturity, these become crusty and disintegrate, freeing their spores.

Habitat
Found on rotting stumps, logs and leaf litter.

The largest of all slime molds—one particularly large specimen was compared by mycologist Sam Ristich to "the vomit of 6 Great Danes."

Fruiting Body: 1–12"

Scrambled Egg Slime

May-Oct.

Wolf's Milk Slime
Lycogala epidendrum

Plasmodial stage is pink.

Fruiting bodies: 1/8– 5/8"

Filled with grayish spore powder when mature.

Also called Toothpaste Slime because of the pink goo inside young specimens.

June-Nov.

Wolf's Milk Slime

Pinkish-gray to brown rounded globes; looking like small pink puffballs (In fact, they were formerly and mistakenly listed with the *Lycoperdon!*). They exude a pinkish goo with the consistency of toothpaste. Gray-brown spores grow on the surface.

Habitat
The hemispherical fruiting bodies grow on dead wood—especially well rotted logs or stumps of coniferous or deciduous trees in shady woods.

TITLES OF INTEREST

Arora, D. 1986. *Mushrooms Demystified.* Berkley, CA: Ten Speed Press.

Barron, G. 1999. *Mushrooms of Northeast North America.* Edmonton, AB: Lone Pine Press.

Bessette, A., A. R. and D. W. Fischer. 1997. *Mushrooms of Northeastern North America.* Syracuse, NY: Syracuse University.

Bossenmaier, E. F. 1997. *Mushrooms of the Boreal Forest.* Saskatoon, SK: University of Saskatchewan.

Hudler, G. W. 1998. *Magical Mushrooms, Mischievous Molds.* Princeton, NJ: Princeton University Press.

Kendrick, B. 2017. *The Fifth Kingdom; 4th Edition.* Focus.

Kuo, M. and S. Methven. 2014. *Mushrooms of the Midwest.* University of Illinois.

Lincoff, G. 1984. *The Audubon Society Field Guide to North American Mushrooms.* New York, NY: Knopf.

Marley, G. 2010. *Chanterelle Dreams and Amanita Nightmares; Love, Lore and Mystique of Mushrooms.* Chelsea Green Publishing.

Marrone, T. 2020. *Mushrooms of the Upper Midwest; 2nd Edition.* Cambridge, MN: Adventure Publications.

Miller Jr., O. K., and H. H. Miller. 2006. *North American Mushrooms.* Gilford, CT: Falcon Guide.

Phillips, R. 2005. *Mushrooms and other Fungi of North America.* Buffalo, NY: Firefly Books.

Schaechter, E. 1998. *In the Company of Mushrooms.* Cambridge, MA: Harvard University Press.

Smith, A. H. 1981. *How to Know Non-Gilled Mushrooms.* New York, NY: Wm. Brown.

Smith, A. H., H. V. Smith and N. Weber. 1979. *How to Know the Gilled Mushrooms.* Dubuque, IA: Wm. C. Brown.

Tekeila, S. 1993. *Start Mushrooming.* Cambridge, MN: Adventure Publications.

CLUBS, MAGAZINES & WEBSITES

Minnesota Mycological Society
www.minnesotamushrooms.org

The Wisconsin Mycological Society
www.wisconsinmycologicalsociety.org

Michigan Mushroom Hunters Club
www.michiganmushroomhunters.org

Northstate Mycological Club
Northeast Wisconsin
www.northstatemycologicalclub.org

Tom Volk's Fungus of the Month
www.TomVolkFungi.net

MykoWeb
Mushrooms, Fungi, Mycology
www.mykoweb.com

Photos of Fungi
www.mycolog.com

Mycologist Michael Kuo's website
www.MushroomExpert.com

Online Identification
www.mycokey.com

Mushroom, The Journal
www.MushroomTheJournal.com

Fungi Magazine
www.FungiMagazine.com
bbunyard@wi.rr.com

GLOSSARY

adnate: Gills attached to the stalk without a notch.

adnexed: Gills attached to the stalk with a notch.

annular Zone: A poorly defined ring on the stalk.

annulus: A ring on the stalk.

apex: The uppermost portion of the stalk.

apendiculate: With pieces of the veil hanging along the margin.

ascomycetes: A major group of fungi that includes those species that produce ascospores in asci (sacs).

ascospore: Spore formed within an ascus (sac).

ascus: A sac-like structure where the ascospores are formed. (*asci*: plural)

asexual: Cells are body parts not resulting from fertilization.

attached: Gills joined to the stalk.

basal: Located at the base of a structure such as a stalk.

basidiomycetes: A major group of fungi that includes those species that produce spores borne on a basidium.

basidiospore: A spore formed on a basidium.

basidium: A club-shaped structure where the spores are formed in. (*basidia*: plural)

basidiomycetes: Such as gilled mushrooms.

bracket: Shelflike fruiting body produced by wood-rotting basidiomycetes.

bruising: Changing color when handled.

button: The immature stage of a mushroom.

clavate: Club-shaped.

coniferous: Cone-bearing.

conk: A large, woody, hoof-shaped polypore growing on wood.

corrugated: Wrinkled, usually with long wavelike ridges.

cortina: Spiderweb-like growth from stalk to cap.

crenate: With uniform rounded lobes; refers to margin of cap.

cristate: Fine branching tips as in some coral fungi.

cup: The saclike tissue at the stalk base left by the universal veil after it has ruptured of some mushrooms.

cuticle: The outermost tissue layer of the cap; skin.

decurrent: Gills that descend or run down the stalk.

deliquesce: Liquify; as in the gills of the genus Coprinus.

disc: The central area of the surface of a mushroom cap.

duff: The partially decayed plant material on the forest floor.

egg: The immature button stage of amanitas and stinkhorns.

fairy Ring: An arc or circle of gilled mushrooms or puffballs arising from a mycelium that expands outward from a central point.

fibril: A tiny fiber.

filiform: Thread-like.

flesh: The inner tissue of a fruiting body.

fluted: Having sharp-cornered ridges extending down the stalk.

free: Gills that are not attached to the stalk.

fruiting body: The fleshy to hard reproductive structure of a fungus, commonly called a mushroom.

GLOSSARY

fusiform: Spindle-shaped; tapering at both ends.

gasteromycetes: A group of Basidiomycetes, such as puffballs, which produce spores in closed chambers within the fruiting body.

glabrous: Bald and smooth.

gleba: Spore-bearing tissue of stinkhorns.

globose: Round; globe-like.

gregarious: Closely scattered over a small area.

heartwood: The inner, usually dead wood, of a tree trunk.

hirsute: Covered with a dense layer of long stiff hairs.

humus: Partially decomposed plant material.

hypha (hyphae): Thread-like filaments of fungi.

inner veil: Another name for partial veil.

lamella: A gill on the underside of the cap of a mushroom.

latex: A watery or milk-like fluid that exudes from some mushrooms when they are cut or bruised.

lignicolous: Growing on wood.

lubricous: Smooth and slippery.

mycelium: A mass of hyphae, typically hidden in a substrate.

mycology: The scientific study of fungi.

mycorrhizal: Having a mutually beneficial relationship with a tree or other plant.

myxomycota: Division of fungi containing the slime molds.

ovate: Shaped like an egg.

ovoid: Somewhat egg-shaped.

parasite: An organism that obtains its nutrients from a living host.

partial veil: A layer of fungal tissue that covers the gills or pores (under the cap) of some immature mushrooms.

pedicels: Slender stalks.

pileus: The cap of the mushroom fruiting body.

piriform: Pear-shaped.

plasmodium: The vegetative stage of a slime mold.

plicate: Deeply grooved, sometimes pleated or folded.

pores: The open ends of the tubes of a bolete or polypore.

pore surface: The undersurface of the cap of a bolete or polypore, where the open ends of the tubes are visible.

pubescent: Having short, soft, downy hairs.

punctate: Marked with tiny points, dots, scales or spots.

putrescent: Soon decaying.

radial: Pointed away from a common central point, like the spokes of a wheel.

recurved: Curved backward or downward.

reticulate: Covered with a net-like pattern of ridges.

rhizomorph: A group of thick, rope-like strands of hyphae growing together as a single organized unit.

rimose: Having distinct cracks or crevices.

ring: Remnants of a partial veil that remain attached to the stalk after the veil ruptures.

saccate: Sheath-like or cup-shaped.

saprophyte: An organism that lives off dead or decaying matter.

sapwood: The living, outer layer of a tree trunk.

scabers: Small, stiff, granular points on the surface of the stalks of some mushrooms.

scabrous: Rough, with short rigid projections.

scale: An erect, flattened, or recurved projection or torn portion of the cap or stalk surface.

sessile: Fruiting bodies that lack a stalk.

setaceous: Stalk with bristles.

serrate: Jagged or toothed like a saw blade.

sexual: Pertaining to fertilization involving two compatible cells.

shelflike (stalkless): Typically growing from wood; usually horizontal, like a shelf.

sinuate: Gills that gradually narrow and become concave near the stalk.

spathulate: Spoon-shaped.

spines: Tapered, downward-pointing projections on the undersurface of some mushroom caps.

sporangium: A sac-like microscopic structure in which asexual spores are produced.

spore: A microscopic reproductive cell with the ability to germinate and form hyphae.

spore case: A structure containing the spore mass in species of Gasteromycetes.

squamose: Having scales.

stalk: The structure that arises from the substrate and supports the cap or spore case of a mushroom; also called stem or stipe.

stellate: Starlike.

stipe: The stalk or stem that supports a mushroom.

striate: Having small, more or less parallel lines or furrows.

strigose: Coated with long, coarse, stiff hairs.

sulcate: Grooved.

subdecurrant: Gills extending slightly down the stalk.

substrate: Organic matter that serves as a food source for a fungal mycelium.

superficial: Merely resting on the surface; not attached.

superior ring: A ring located on the upper stalk surface.

symbiont: An organism that lives in a mutually beneficial relationship, or symbiosis, with another organism.

terrestrial: Growing on the ground.

truncate: Appearing cut off at the end.

umbo: A pointed or rounded elevation a the center of a mushroom cap.

uniseriate: Arranged in a single row.

universal veil: A layer of fungal tissue that completely encloses immature stages of some mushrooms.

veil: A layer of fungal tissue that covers all or part of some immature mushrooms

ventricose: Swollen at the middle.

vermiform: Wormlike.

verrucose: Warty.

villose: Coated with long, tiny, soft hairs.

viscid: Sticky or tacky.

volva: A typically cup-like sac that remains around the base of a mushroom stalk when the universal veil ruptures.

warts: Small patches of tissue that remain on the top of a mushroom cap when the universal veil ruptures.

INDEX

OTHER FINE REGIONAL
KOLLATH-STENSAAS BOOKS

**Amazing Agates
Lake Superior's
Banded Gemstone**
Scott Wolter

**Rock Picker's Guide
to Lake Superior's
North Shore**
Mark Sparky Stensaas

**Earthworms
of the Great Lakes**
Cindy Hale

**Amphibians &
Reptiles of MN,
WI & MI**
Allen Blake Sheldon

**Butterflies
of the
North Woods**
2nd edition
Larry Weber

**Damselflies
of MN, WI
& MI**
Bob DuBois

**Dragonflies
of the
North Wood**
3rd edition
Kurt Mead

**Insects
of the
North Woods**
Jeffrey Hahn

**Lichens
of the
North Woods**
Joe Walewski

**Mammals
of the
North Woods**
Jim Sogaard

**Orchids
of the
North Woods**
Kim & Cindy Risen

**Spiders
of the
North Woods**
2nd edition
Larry Weber

**Ferns
of the
North Woods**
Joe Walewski

Find out more at **KollathStensaas.com**